Smarter
Than You Think

*Accessing Your Personal Powers
to Triumph in College*

Suzanne Liff

outskirts
press

For Grandma Celia and Grandma Dora
and my mother, Doris Ashinoff Brandell

Table of Contents

ACKNOWLEDGEMENTS

The seeds of this book were planted many years ago in my early days as a resource room teacher in a public school district on Long Island. Inspired by collaboration with my colleague, school psychologist Dr. Susan Rubenstein, I conceived the creation of a book called "The Affective Side of Learning." Susan and I would talk and talk about the emotional aspects of each student in our trust. It was apparent that their social and emotional makeup was what differentiated them the most, and impacted how they saw and negotiated the world, in and out of school. And so it is, through preschool to college. I will never forget the imprint of those early chats.

Fast forward to today. Much appreciation goes to Nassau Community College for awarding and affording me the sabbatical time to actually begin the formal writing of this book. I am grateful to friends and colleagues there, for their participation at my seminars on social and emotional intelligence, responses to surveys that gathered their insights and points of view on students' experiences and behaviors, and for their overall encouragement on this project.

Of course, this book is primarily for and about college students. I have been in the company of these fabulous creatures for many years. They have shown me so much about the aspirations, trials, challenges and victories of their lives and times while in school. I am impressed by their openness, courage and hearts, and remain grateful to know, teach them, and to learn from them.

To bring this work to fruition, I am lucky to have become a part of the Outskirts Press team. In particular, I thank my author representative, Jennifer Rush, for her guidance and support.

My son, Dr. Jeremy Liff, has always been an inspiration to me, in both heart and mind. Brilliant in many ways, he epitomizes SEI in his perseverance, grit, empathy, and warmth. I am forever blessed by his love and support.

Most of all here, I want to thank my partner and friend, Dr. Allan Levin, for his love and ongoing interest in the development of this book. His willingness to always listen to the latest revision, his commentary, and personal embrace of SEI as one of his own mantras, made the creative process gentler and kinder for me. I am ever grateful.

Where This Book Takes You

I can't wait for you to know, and deeply understand, the message of this book. Most students head to college totally without it. You won't be one of them.

Your success in college is not just about your academic skills and strengths. Nope, it's not about how great you read, how well you do math, or if your IQ is off the charts.

A large part of how you do in school, the outcomes you achieve and the experiences you take away, are dependent upon qualities in you that probably have never been tested, scored, or given a grade. Yet they have always been operative in your educational life, and will continue to be.

In the coming pages, you will learn that there are many ways to be smart. Some reflect your intelligence and cognitive abilities. Others include your athletic, musical, or even spiritual capacities. But the most encompassing ones, shadowing you wherever you go, are not measured on achievement tests, writing samples, or at auditions.

They are your personal capacities; those that constitute what are sometimes called your personal intelligences. These include truly knowing yourself and your needs, being able to soothe your moods, adjust your reactions, set and pursue your goals, know how you are doing, hang on when you feel like quitting, and connect positively with others.

You likely have no idea how relevant these personal abilities are to your academic success and your happiness throughout your college years. They are supremely powerful. They can help you become the "smartest" person in the room, whether or not you get straight A's or have the highest IQ.

Even if you typically do well academically, learning about and nurturing your personal competencies will have a great impact on how you experience college. Recognizing and strengthening these abilities can enhance your enjoyment of classes, help you deal with the pressures to get good grades, enrich the way you socialize and form relationships, and generally improve your well being and contentment during your time in school.

The measures that make up your IQ are generally stable throughout your life. You are born "that way." The components of your personal intelligence, often known as your emotional intelligence (EQ) or social and emotional intelligence (SEI), evolve over your lifetime. You are not yet the best you can be. You are still growing! And you can leverage that process.

Get ready to discover, develop and strengthen the amazing components of your social and emotional self. You will learn how they improve almost every aspect of your college life, from managing the work load to relating to your professors, completing your assignments on time, studying in ways that work, enriching how you socialize and forge relationships, and dealing with missteps or even occasional failures that are part of the college experience.

Focus directly on yourself as you read this book. Stop and consider how the ideas relate to you personally. They all do.

Let's take this important intrapersonal journey together. Find out all about your personal powers and how to access them to triumph in college. And yes, you will discover that you have the capacity to be smarter than you think!

CHAPTER 1

Warm Up: Pumping Your Personal Powers

"Even though the future seems far away, it is actually beginning right now."

— *Mattie Stepanek, poet and motivational speaker*

I was a hippie in college…well, sort of. I wasn't totally out there, but did go off to school with the words, *Peace* and *Love* painted on my car and decals of flowers pasted along the fender.

I remember walking into my dorm room on that first day and thinking my roommate was totally cool. Over her bed she had hung a poster that said, "Today is the first day of the rest of your life." It had a pink, yellow, and orange sky in the background, robust with the booming rays of a tropical sunrise. At the time, it felt magical. Inspirational quotes on posters were not that common then. The message seemed very profound and important to me. You could always start over.

Every day could be a new beginning, a fresh start. No matter what had come before, today you could reboot. The rest of your life lay ahead. There would always be new possiblities...for as long as you lived. Wow! I recalled those thoughts many times throughout my college years.

I sometimes recount this awakening to my students. And now I share it with you. You're at a new beginning of your life...at least when it comes to your education. You might have recently graduated from high school or will very soon. Did you just start college? Maybe you will begin in a while, or you're seriously thinking about applying. It's possible that you stepped away from school for some years and have decided to try again.

Today college is a destination for more students than ever. Freshman come in all shapes and sizes. One is 17 years old with a new driver's license and another is a grandpa who has been driving since before there were car phones! Some entering students were at the top of their class in high school, and others just managed to pass and earn their diploma. Students come from families where everyone attended college for many generations. Others are the first in their family to pursue a college degree. Many begin college with strong academic skills, athletic abilities or other talents and interests. They were on the honor roll or even class valedictorian. Others didn't excel quite so well. They struggled through the high school years and couldn't wait to be finished with school. Now they recognize the benefits of a college degree and want to go for it.

No matter the back story, people generally believe that getting through college is directly related to being smart and having strong academic skills. The higher your IQ and the better you can think, read, write, or do math, then the more likely you are to succeed in higher education. Right?

Well, not entirely. There is no doubt that being intelligent and academically capable is an advantage in college. For sure, these are resources that enable you to tackle college material, think critically, question, and even enjoy the learning process.

But they are not everything. While many students who are intellectually strong do well, some do not succeed or choose to quit college. Other students who begin college with some limitations in their reading and writing or without the highest intellectual indicators, do go on to succeed and really shine in college.

How is that possible?

Here's what you should know, and what this book is all about.

Much of your learning in school is rooted within your emotional brain. Learning is personal. Your capacity to thrive, flourish and grow academically is as deeply connected to the strength of your social and emotional self as it is to your intelligence or the academic skills you have achieved. How well you do in college is not just about how "smart" you are and what you know. As important is "who" you are; how you think about yourself, how you approach, manage, frame, execute, and persist on the tasks you confront, and how you relate to the people around you in your college world.

Knowing about and understanding something called social and emotional intelligence, or SEI, can lead to joy and academic success in college. Briefly put, for now, social and emotional intelligence is a combination of abilities that allows you to recognize, identify, understand, and manage your emotions, personally and with others. You can use these abilities to reason and solve problems. [1, 2] Your awareness of your SEI, your ability to call upon it, and, yes, grow it, will have a huge impact on your life as a college student. It will help you rise in school, both in and out of the classroom.

As a professor, I am passionate about the importance of social and emotional intelligence. I know how much it affects the way students behave in and out of class and succeed - or fail - on assignments and exams. SEI can be the barometer for whether or not a person enjoys their entire college experience. Frankly, most students start college without a clue about the importance of SEI.

Your SEI is like your mobile home. If you were a turtle, it would be your shell. Wherever you go, there it is! SEI sets a foundation for all learning; for setting your goals, for managing the many challenges that come along, and for keeping you going when you may feel like quitting.

This doesn't mean that your intellectual strengths and past accomplishments don't matter. Of course they do. Entering college with a strong fund of scholarly skills and other abilities certainly *is* an advantage. When you start a new class, your capacity to read and comprehend, write well, and have a strong vocabulary will go a long way. Being able to think critically or outside the box will enrich your involvement in coursework and make your studies interesting and enjoyable. Having good technical skills is also a plus. The more information literate you are, the easier it will be for you to access knowledge and research. If you are creative or artistic, perform on stage, or excel athletically, these strengths can be put to great use in school, in class and in outside activities. And the more you strengthen and apply your skills, the better. I hope that in college you build your scholarship and inquisitive mind and feel joy losing yourself in your talents and interests. There's nothing like it.

Yet strength in academics and having talent in particular areas doesn't guarantee your success in college. Conversely, limits in skill sets or academic ability is not always the reason students fail. Something more personal is also at work.

A large portion of your success and happiness in school; your capacity to thrive in your classes, to manage all your coursework, set goals, deal with problems and setbacks, to feel safe and connected on campus, and to persist while others may give up, rests in your abilities to function well as a socially and emotionally capable person.

Studies have shown that most of our life success in all different arenas - almost 80% of it, is dependent upon social and emotional intelligence. As much as 50% of success in school emerges from being a socially and emotionally capable person.[3]

In a recent informal survey of community college professors, the majority believed that students who failed or did poorly in class did so **not** because the academic demands were too high or beyond those students' abilities. Rather, it was limitations in personal competencies and qualities that led those students to fail or drop out.[4]

Together, we will dig deeply into social and emotional intelligence. It is a combination of several components that you can enrich and strengthen. We will focus on how these find their way into almost every challenge, exchange, and demand of your college experience... in the classroom, on the campus, when you are alone and with your friends. It's amazing!

You will consider how you can grow your understanding and use of social and emotional intelligence to help you throughout school. You will see how the outcomes of the circumstances and situations you face will be directly related to how you personally respond to and manage them.

Enjoy discovering the factors that make up your personal learning. They can enable you to succeed, even when times are tough and you may feel like giving up. *Intend* to make them part of your college life as you strive for success in your coursework and have more fun and satisfaction in your relationships and activities. *Intention* is the first step to getting where you want to go!

As you read, stop and think personally...all about your-self. You might want to jot down some of your own thoughts and reflections at the conclusion of each chapter in the Consider This Box. Just so you know..... writing helps you think, realize your personal views, and express them in your own voice.

Step by step, let's uncover the foundation of your success in college. Access your personal powers. Get ready to triumph!

Consider This: What personal qualities do you think it takes to succeed in college? List three or four. Which of the qualities do you possess? Which would you like to strengthen or develop? Write about these here.

CHAPTER 2

So Many Ways to Be Smart: Multiple Intelligences and You

"Promise me you'll always remember: You're braver than you believe, and stronger than you seem, and smarter than you think."

— *A.A. Milne, from his book* Winnie the Pooh

Mario attended a high school program for students with special needs. He and his classmates had a lot of potential, but also a variety of learning differences that made reading, writing, or doing math a challenge. Mario struggled tackling all of the books that were required reading for his 11th grade English class. He rarely completed his writing assignments. He had a hard time staying focused on any text he attempted to absorb. Sometimes this caused him to call out, tap on his desk, or talk to other students during class. This would disrupt the lesson and led to his being reprimanded by his teacher on a regular basis. He often landed in after-school detention.

In amazing contrast, Mario could paint a picture that would knock your socks off. His use of color and mastery of design was remarkable. His style was pure Mario.....intense color, abstraction of forms, unique connections among his whimsical figures. His paintings livened up the walls of our classroom, as well as some of the halls in the high school.

In the spring, several classes in the school participated in a service learning project. When it came time to select a student who would teach art to a special group of middle school students, Mario was our man. Known as a "behavioral problem" in academic classes, Mario was clear, patient, convivial, deliberate and gentle when he taught younger students to apply paint to canvas. The kids loved him. The art gallery that was created under his guidance took everyone's breath away. Though reading and writing tortured him, with brush in hand - rather than a pen or word processor - Mario was a master.

––––––—◦(◦)◦—––––––

Our world is full of people who excel in certain areas, yet struggle or function at a much lower level in others. This helps us understand that, indeed, there are many ways to be smart. Entrepreneurs Barbara Corcoran in real estate and Richard Branson in aviation, comedian Whoopi

Goldberg, actors Daniel Radcliff and Tom Cruise, film director Steven Spielberg, and NFL quarterback Tim Tebow, are all said to have dyslexia and were, or still are, challenged by reading and writing. Even renowned people like inventor Thomas Edison, scientist Albert Einstein, and Beatles musician John Lennon were dyslexic. Yet they all went on to be celebrated for their talents and abilities in other areas. They made exceptional contributions to our culture and society.

People are complex and very different. Each person has a variety of ways in which he or she is strong and can even excel. And you will soon see how excelling in capacities that have to do with social and emotional skills is also a kind of intelligence. It is one that has a global impact on our ability to come shining though in many of life's challenges.

Before we go on, let's build some background knowledge about the concept of intelligence, and see how it has evolved. This will help you understand how being socially and emotionally smart can exist as an intelligence in and of itself.

A Brief Look at IQ

Most everyone has heard of IQ, short for intelligence quota. Though it's an actual statistical measure, IQ has come to be used in a casual way to designate how "smart" someone is. (Is that your IQ or your shoe size?) We think, having a "high" IQ is good and a low IQ, not so good.

Actually, IQ is a concept that was developed by French psychologist, Alfred Binet and a colleague over a century ago in the early 1900's. They wanted to identify students who might need assistance in school. Binet found that when they were asked questions, some students responded as though they were older than their actual age, while others answered questions as a younger child might. Binet created a measure of intelligence based on calculations comparing an individual's "mental age" with their true age. Multiplying the comparison by 100 yielded the "IQ" score.

Later, used and adapted in the United States at Stanford University, the renamed "Stanford Intelligence Scale" became the basis for intelligence testing for years to come.[1] You may have taken a form of the test during your public school years.

The test results in a numerical score, falling within a particular range that is compared to the average. For example, scores between 90 and 110 would be considered average. Scores above or below these marks would indicate higher or lower potential. Revised versions of the Stanford-Binet exam have been used routinely in schools, and extensively by the military to help place soldiers in various roles in the armed forces.

But even Binet had concerns about assigning one single number to portray a person's entire intellectual potential. Over the years, researchers and educators came to understand that a person's intelligence is a composite of several capacities.

Perhaps you were administered an assessment of cognition called the "Wechsler Intelligence Scale." It is considered a more meaningful measure of a person's abilities. That is because it evaluates intelligence in ten or fifteen areas. These relate to factors including memory, processing speed (how quickly one can learn), language, and reasoning ability.[2]

Over the last four decades, Harvard psychologist Howard Gardner has helped shape our view of intellectual potential with his theory of multiple intelligences. Yes, that's plural. It helps us understand that there are many ways to be "smart."

Below is a listing of the intelligences depicted in Dr. Gardner's works [3,4,5], with a short description for each. As you read through these, think about yourself. Consider the various ways **you** are intelligent. You don't always need formal testing to recognize your own abilities and how you might excel. Knowing these capacities, and thinking about how they apply to you, strengthens your understanding of yourself; your self-awareness. This kind of personal knowledge can serve you well as a student.

Pay special attention to the personal intelligences toward the end of the list. These forge the basis of social and emotional intelligence, our focus going forward. We will discuss them in detail as we move on.

Gardner's Capacities of Multiple Intelligence

Linguistic: The Intelligence of Words and Language
Think of civil rights leader Martin Luther King Jr., Harry Potter author J.K. Rowling, and former President Barack Obama

This ability involves sensitivity to language, both spoken and written. It includes the capacity to express yourself effectively and articulately and comprehend or receive language that you hear or read. Having a strong vocabulary is part of this capacity.

As a student, linguistic intelligence helps you understand lectures and your reading materials, write papers, speak well, and communicate in and out of class.

Logical/Mathematical: The Intelligence of Numbers and Reasoning
Think of scientists and physicists Albert Einstein, Steven Hawking, and Sir Isaac Newton and business and tech entrepreneurs Steve Jobs and Jeff Bezos

This capacity includes analyzing problems logically and carrying out mathematical operations and scientific investigations.

Strength here will certainly help you through your math and science classes. But logical thinking and problem solving finds its way into many subject areas. When combined with linguistic skills, it supports students through solution building tasks, test taking and research, computer sciences and technology.

Spatial: The Intelligence of Imagery
Think of artists Pablo Picasso, Andy Warhol, and architect Frank Lloyd Wright

This is skill in recognizing, creating and manipulating patterns in a space. Highly visual, it includes the capacity to form mental images, perceive dimension and details, and visualize objects in relationship to one another.

Artists, architects, sculptors, designers, pilots and navigators call upon this capacity in their work. Perceiving the location of the buildings on your campus and parallel parking your car in the lot without hitting the curb takes a bit of spatial intelligence!

Musical: The Intelligence of Rhythm and Tone
Think of singer/song writers Drake, Taylor Swift, and John Legend and classical composers Mozart, Beethoven, and Chopin

This reflects skill in the performance, composition, arrangement and appreciation of musical patterns.

You can recognize this intelligence in your favorite musicians, groups, composers, or performers. Perhaps you see it in yourself, or know others who have great "rhythm." Some people call this a talent. Gardener feels strongly that ability here be considered a kind of intelligence.

Bodily-Kinesthetic: The Intelligence of Body and Hands; Movement and Coordination
Think of athletes LeBron James, Serena Williams, Peyton Manning and Michael Jordan

This is the ability to use one's body adeptly through movement, or learn and solve problems through physical sensation.

Athleticism is forged through this intelligence, as any sports fan can attest. But this intelligence also helps a person be mechanically inclined; or work well with their hands as in the case of a surgeon, yoga instructor, craftsperson, jeweler or technician.

Naturalist: The Intelligence of the Natural World
Think of anthropologist/primotologist Jane Goodall, conservationist Rachel Carson, naturalist John Muir, and photographer Ansel Adams

This ability involves a sensitivity to the natural world and an appreciation of its features. It includes a calling to be amid nature or the outdoors; to see, feel, touch, and interact with the environment, the earth, plants, and animals.

Naturalist intelligence may draw someone to work as an environmentalist or wildlife conservationist; to be drawn to work in the fields, outdoors, perhaps as a botanist or landscape architect, or study the stars and the universe, as an astronomer or physicist.

Existential: The Intelligence of Our Existence
Think of Jesus Christ, the Dalai Lama, Buddha, and Mother Teresa

Connected to spirituality, this capacity involves conceptualizing intangible experiences and phenomena, going beyond the sensory or physical realm. So this capacity relates to considering the universe, our purpose for existence, life and death and beyond.

Sometimes referred to as "cosmic" intelligence, those with existential intelligence will tackle questions that are vast, deep, and possibly without a definitive answer. Why are we born? Do we ever die? What is our soul? Is there evil? In college, you might find yourself delving into questions such as these in theology or philosophy classes.

The Personal Intelligences
· ·

Interpersonal: The Intelligence of
Socialization and Perceptivity of Others

*Think of psychiatrist Sigmund Freud, psychologist
Dr. Phil, and TV personality Oprah Winfrey*

This capacity refers to a person's ability to recognize
and understand others, including their intentions, motivations, feelings and desires. It embraces a capacity
to empathize, care, relate to others well, and communicate effectively.

People with interpersonal intelligence tend to work,
play, and interact well with friends and colleagues.
So this intelligence fosters positive relationships in all
walks of life and professions.

This intelligence might lead you take classes in the
social sciences, including psychology, sociology, or in
areas such as criminal justice, communications, and
even advertising and marketing. If you have height-
ened interpersonal intelligence, you might choose a
career that involves strong "people skills" and connection to others. These include teacher, psychologist,
counselor, or physician. The best salespeople tend to
have well developed interpersonal skills.

Intrapersonal: The Intelligence of Self Knowledge

Think of philosophers Aristotle, Confucius, and writer Deepak Chopra

Intra at the beginning of a word means "inside of" or "within." Intrapersonal intelligence is the capacity to understand oneself; to look inward, be introspective and self-reflective. It involves being in touch with your own thoughts, emotions, behaviors, ways of thinking, and motivations.

Intrapersonal intelligence helps us understand the reasons behind our actions and why we feel the way we do. It supports the capacity to soothe ourself when troubled, adjust our thinking and behavior when necessary, make decisions that we feel comfortable with, and develop positive ways to pursue individual happiness.

In school, many of the social sciences address topics that involve intrapersonal intelligence. Courses in other areas of study too, such as philosophy, theology, diversity, and gender studies, will consider related issues.

What About You?

Where do you see yourself regarding these capacities? Go back over each intelligence and comment about yourself in the margin. How do you evaluate yourself in each area?

Having a handle on your "intelligences" gives you a jumpstart as a college student. This knowledge about yourself can help you come up with the most effective ways to learn and study, choose courses wisely, and articulate your needs to professors and counselors clearly and meaningfully. We will take a deeper look at understanding your own learning strengths and preferences in Chapter 4.

Gardner was not the first researcher to recognize the personal intelligences, nor is he the last. More than ever, scientists, psychologists, and educators are acknowledging the significance of personal, emotional, and social capabilities for success in school, as well as in the workplace and in our personal lives. [6, 7, 8]

But you are thinking about your life in college. Let's focus on how the personal intelligences; ways to be "smart" socially and emotionally, can make a world of difference in your college experience and how you succeed-both in and out of the classroom. Read on.

Consider This: In which of the intelligences are you strongest? How might this impact your decisions about your future studies or career? Jot down your thoughts.

CHAPTER 3

SEI: What Is It and Why Does it Matter So Much?

"Emotional Intelligence is the difference that makes the difference."

— J.D. Meier, author

"There is no separation of mind and emotions; emotions, thinking, and learning are all linked."

— Eric Jensen, educator and author

What do we mean by social and emotional intelligence... and what does it have to do with you
as a college student? Let me begin by telling you about
my experience at a conference I attended recently. As
do all professionals, educators, including teachers and
professors, continue to develop their skills and understanding about their work throughout their careers.

They study how students learn best and how best to teach. In addition to reading about these in journals and books, they may take classes and attend seminars to strengthen their teaching practices and stay current on important matters and trends in education. They learn from one another.

I was presenting at such a gathering. I asked my audience of college professors to help create an imaginary "Ad" to bring students to their campus. It looked something like this:

Wanted: Successful College Student

Must be _____, _____, and _____.

Those who _____, _____, and _____ need not apply.

The professors were to fill in the blanks and then discuss their responses. You might go ahead and fill in the blanks now from your own point of view. What do you think it takes to be a successful student in college? What do you think would be undesirable qualities, so you would encourage that those people not apply? Take a moment to fill in the Want Ad yourself right now.

Of course, the first three blanks call for qualities professors would like to see in their students. The next three represent those not so wanted! What do you think the professors at the conference said?

You might automatically think professors asked for really "smart" students; that they wanted "brainy" students who know all the answers and could solve all sorts of problems. They would want students to be great readers, writers, and thinkers.

OK...intellectual potential and academic skills *do* matter, and certainly can help make life easier and interesting for both the student and the professor. However, that isn't what most professors said. And maybe it isn't what you said.

Professors filled in the first blanks with words such as:

- highly motivated
- hardworking
- interested in the subject I teach and asks questions
- on time and comes to class regularly
- organized
- willing to get help if they need it
- able to enjoy my class
- use what I teach them in a meaningful way

For those who "need not apply," they responded with comments like: are lazy, have a negative attitude, don't put in the time to complete assignments, are not open to learning new ideas or thinking for themselves, are disruptive or inattentive, disorganized, miss class, are disrespectful. [1]

I decided to present a similar activitity to groups of students at a freshman college seminar. Can you believe that almost all the students filled in the blanks exacly like the professors! How about you?

Those professors, and those insightful students, understood that success in college is not dependent on having a high IQ or being at the top of the achievement ladder in reading, writing and math.

Intuitively, they knew that other factors related to attitude, interest, commitment and behavior have a huge impact on a positive and successful college experience. These factors are part of a group of capacities we call social and emotional intelligence, also known as SEI.

You will soon see how they build the foundation for your success in college, both academically and socially.

The Meaning of SEI

Many researchers, including Daniel Goleman, Peter Salovey and John Mayer have helped us understand the meaning of social and emotional intelligence. Here is an adapted version of what they say....

Social and emotional intelligence involves the ability to recognize and appraise our own feelings and the feelings of others. It is the capacity to express emotion; the ability to understand emotion in others, and the ability to manage and regulate emotion well in ourselves and our relationships. We use this capacity to motivate ourselves in our pursuits and to promote emotional and intellectual growth. [2,3]

When you think deeply about these words, you can't help but realize how important SEI is to your day to day existence. It impacts your life and experiences as a member of your family, as a friend, and as a colleague or co-worker. Especially for our conversation here, it profoundly affects your well-being as a student. The way you flourish in school is very much dependent upon you social and emotional intelligence. Research suggests that emotional and social capacities are not only important in helping students transition from high school to college, but in how they adapt, manage stress, persist and thrive throughout the college years.[4]

It's Organic!

A wonderful thing about SEI is that it develops over time....and it can keep on growing! So your social and emotional competencies right now aren't as strong as they could be in the future! Not only that, you can help them grow. If you decide to be conscious of your social and emotional self, and its role in the comings and goings of your college life, you can make real positive changes in your life. This will impact the way you see and understand yourself, manage your emotions and your relationships with others, and handle your responsibilities. These are major determinants of how well you do in school. Going further, your strengths in social and emotional intelligence will affect how you will succeed in your job or profession, in the community, and in all of your relationships to come.

But whoa....you're headed for or are in school. So let's find out more about SEI and how it will work to make your college life so much better.

Six Factors of Social and Emotional Intelligence.... and their place in your campus life

Your social and emotional intelligence is a composite of six important factors. Here is a brief go-round to introduce you to the terms that identify them.[5] The quotation that follows each helps you immediately see its application to the world of college. We'll spend a lot more time looking at these factors in the coming pages.

Self-Awareness: Your capacity to recognize and name your emotions, and to understand their triggers.

"This is my first day in my first class. How am I feeling now? Why am I feeling this way?

Regulation of Emotions: The capacity to manage your impulses and your mood.

"OMG...I'm freaking out over the number of pages I need to review in sociology. Let me take some deep breaths and come up with a reading schedule so that I am finished by Tuesday."

Goal Setting: The ability to set your sights on an outcome you want and the capacity to harness your emotions to get there.

"My dream is to become a physical therapist and no matter how long it takes, and how hard the coursework. I will do what I must to get that credential."

Self-Monitoring: The capacity to judge how you are doing and make adjustments along the way so you can better reach your objective.

"Wow...I thought I was finished studying but I realized I hadn't covered the last chapter on the economic impact of the Civil War on manufacturers

in the North. I will need to pass on going out tonight."

Empathy: The ability to be aware of and understand the feelings of others.

"Professor O'Connor seemed really upset when I came in late to class yesterday. I think he felt badly that I missed the whole introduction to the lesson. I will really try to make it on time from now on."

Social Skills: The ability to form and maintain positive relationships.

"My first day on campus I didn't know a soul, and now I have at least three or four people who I can call a good friend."

———— ◉ ————

Awareness of your own needs and feelings, your capacity to regulate your emotions, the ability to set goals and monitor yourself along the way to reach them, having empathy for others and establishing meaningful social relationships will have tremendous impact on your academic life and personal experiences on campus. *Together, these qualities can transform your college experience.*

As you get to know and understand these social and

emotional capacities, and personalize them, you will become more and more powerful in adapting, adjusting, and structuring your world on campus. You will develop resources and strength to manage situations, confront adversities, and modulate your reactions. You will become more open to new opportunities, and stay afloat when you face difficulties.

Challenge is inevitable. Failing or getting knocked down is a possibility. But remember, as anyone from Tiger Woods to Demi Lovato would tell you, it's the getting up that counts. Social and emotional intelligence can give you the stamina to do so, and to construct your life in such a way that the falls are less likely to happen. When they do, you will be better able to manage the pain and move forward, grow, and enjoy the journey along the way.

In the following chapters, you will learn more about each of the six factors, and how they really, really, *really* can help you rise up in college.

Consider This: Go back over the SEI capacities. Which do you think is your strongest one right now? How so? What would you like to strengthen for the future? Why? Write about each of these.

CHAPTER 4

Look Inside: Being Grounded and Self-Aware

"There is in you something that waits and listens for the sound of the genuine in yourself."

— *Howard Thurman, author, theologian, civil rights leader*

"How are you?" This is probably the question most asked of us when we haven't seen or spoken to someone in a while. We tend to answer in a perfunctory manner...."I'm ok," or "Fine," or, "Well, I can't complain."

But really being able to identify and express what we feel can be a lot more complicated, and a lot more meaningful. It takes self-awareness.

Self-awareness is an important component of your social and emotional intelligence. It is being consciously aware of your emotions or moods as they occur. Our moods can change in a heart-beat, based on our circumstances or the events in our lives. Self-awareness involves paying attention to yourself and being in touch with your feelings. Sometimes this capacity is called mindfulness. Self-awareness can help you through a variety of circumstances in college, and of course, in life. To begin thinking about being self-aware in college, let's consider Caryn.

Caryn's Story
. . . .

Caryn staggered into her 8 am English Literature class. Particularly unnerving was that an essay exam was scheduled. But she was exhausted. The night before she had celebrated at her parents' 25th anniversary party with her entire family. To top it off, she had volunteered to drive her cousins to the airport for their "red-eye" flight back to Houston. She didn't get to bed until after 2 am.

Caryn had known she would have a late night before the class. She tried to do the right thing by preparing for the exam over three days before the party.

But all her efforts seemed to fly out the window on test day. As she entered the classroom, her head throbbed. Her heart pounded hard in her chest. She felt really anxious, almost out of control. Making her way to her desk, her brain seemed frozen. She couldn't remember anything about the material she had studied so thoroughly. It's not fair! She started to freak out as the exams were being distributed.

What was happening? What would she do?

Have you ever had an experience similar to Caryn's, where you are overtaken by your emotions? Do you know what makes you anxious? Happy? Calm? Angry? Do you know what triggers these feelings in you? When you think about taking an exam, are you aware of just how stressed you may feel?

Emotions confront us regularly in our daily lives. After waiting ten minutes in the student lot for a parking space and someone swoops into the spot you had targeted, are you aware of how annoyed and angry you may become and how disgruntled you might still feel as you arrive to class 15 minutes late because you had to find another spot? If your friend doesn't show up for a lunch date, are you conscious of how your hurt feelings can impact you while sitting through your history class lesson that follows?

Being self-aware includes self-reflection; looking inward.

It implies having a conscious thought about your internal mood or feeling state. This awareness doesn't make a difficult feeling go away, *but it helps the difficult feelings from taking you away.* It is the first step to having a handle on your emotions, identifying their cause, soothing yourself, and subsequently managing your emotions, rather than being overwhelmed by them.

Let's get back to Caryn. After she sat down at her desk, Caryn smartly took a moment for herself after she received her test booklet. She closed her eyes and took several deep breaths. She consciously slowed down her breathing and reminded herself that yes, she had, in fact, prepared. She visualized herself on her bed, reviewing several short stories and essays for the exam. Slowly she began to recall the titles and authors, the details and thesis of each. She wrote these on the back of the test booklet as they came to mind. She began to relax. Her anxiety subsided. She turned over the exam booklet and read the questions. Her focus shifted and she moved into a zone of connection with the material. She thought and accessed her knowledge, jotted down notes and key ideas, and then began to write her essay. Recognizing her anxiety, Caryn responded to her feelings. She acknowledged them, chose to rid herself of them, took actions to soothe herself, and moved into a better place.

Researchers have helped us understand that self-awareness, being in touch with our mood or emotional state, goes hand in hand with the thoughts we have about that state and then the actions we take to modify how we are feeling. Being self-aware doesn't imply that we are always happy, but that we are at least in touch with our moods, and are potentially in a better position to navigate through our emotions. We trust our capacity to feel ok. For you as a student, it is important to realize that there is a direct relationship with your emotional well-being and positive academic development. [1] Self-awareness is the first step to managing our emotions. We'll explore way of managing or regulating emotions in the next chapter.

Daniel Goleman summarizes three distinctive ways people tend to respond to and deal with their emotions.[2] They are adapted for you in the following scenarios. Think about yourself as you read. Which way characterizes you?

Responding to Your Emotions

Self-Aware: I have a good deal of clarity about my moods. Though I have ups and downs, I trust that I have the capacity to move out of a negative place in a reasonable period of time. I generally feel pretty good and don't feel a sense of inner turmoil or confusion.

Engulfed: I often feel overwhelmed by my emotions and unable to get away from them. My moods control me, rather than me being in charge of my moods. I feel lost in my emotions and helpless to escape them. It's like I have little control over my emotional life and often feel out of control emotionally.

Accepting: I feel a person doesn't control their emotions. They are what they are and so I just accept them.

Interestingly, accepting emotions can work relatively positively or negatively. When a person is usually in a good place, he or she accepts that feeling. There is little motive to change it and all is well. A person can also be conscious of feeling down or in a negative place. If he accepts that state, believing that it there is nothing to do to change it, it can leave him or her feeling depressed or in despair on a regular basis.

Clearly, of these three responses, being self-aware is the most evolved.

———(●)———

Being self-aware as a college student is a wonderful attribute. Having a level of consciousness about how you are feeling and why you feel the way you do is the first step to movement to a better place, and that movement is to your benefit. Recognizing and naming your emotions helps you gain a handle on your feelings. It is then that you can choose to reboot. Also, knowing what triggers your moods can help you make better choices for yourself so that negative feelings are less likely to occur. And if they do, they are likely to dissipate more quickly.

The Benefits of Self-Awareness

Here are some further benefits that evolve from being self-aware.

1. **You understand the reasons and circumstances for your emotions.**

   Say you are feeling stressed out and a bit un-settled as you drive home from your first day of classes. You relate your discomfort to the amount of required reading you have for English 101 this semester. You are overwhelmed and frightened by the number of books that have been assigned and how long they are! You consider yourself a slow reader and have no idea how you will get through all those pages. You can connect your anxiety to something specific. Though it may seem odd at first, yes, that is the good news.

   Being aware of that uncomfortable feeling helps you take several positive steps. You decide to talk to your classmates about the number of books that were assigned. You learn that you are not alone in your worries. You decide to make a reading plan and assign yourself thirty pages of reading every night. You meet with your professor for suggestions on which selections to devote the most time and how to organize the reading. You start to feel less stressed.

It's awful to walk around with a generalized state of anxiety, without knowing really what is setting you off. *Connecting your emotions to something specific can encapsulate the feelings and help you deal with them.* Knowing what sets you off helps you plan better for the next time around. If you know that large quantities of reading material really stresses you out, then you can create a course schedule that doesn't include too many heavily reading laden classes at one time. You can get books on tape. You can block out periods of time to get the reading done.

John's Story

The ability to connect your general mood with the circumstances that trigger it is important while you're in school. Events that occur in your personal life can really seep into your academic life.

I'm reminded of John. He began my reading class really upbeat and involved. He was always seated when I entered our classroom, greeting me with a nod and smile. We were both huge Giants football fans, and often chatted about sports before class began, especially on Monday morning after Sunday's game. John naturally took a leadership role in the small groups formed in class, and was always prepared with assignments.

One day, midway into the semester, he came into class like a different person. (Just the fact that he hadn't been waiting in his seat indicated some kind of change.) He was quiet, almost sullen. He seemed tuned out and distant. He sat with his head crestfallen, gazing at the floor. He no longer contributed to class discussions and stopped turning in his work. Well, I had to ask... so I did one day after class. "Hey...you seem different. Is something the matter?"

Any ideas? Well if you said his girlfriend had broken up with him, you'd be right. They had been together for three years. She had "moved on" and there was no turning back. I really felt for John and his loss, and told him that. I expressed my respect for his sensitivities and shared that, to me, his sadness meant that he was a person who could feel deeply and care for another, and that was a wonderful thing. (I was confident, from my own life experiences and self-awareness, that John would eventually feel better; that the depths of what he was experiencing would dissipate, and with a heart like his, he would find love again. But I didn't think this was the time to say that.)

Mostly, I acknowledged his sadness. I also tried to encourage John to compartmentalize a bit. I suggested he use his time in class and school to give him a break from his sad thoughts. It was ok to be distracted from them. It didn't mean that he wasn't hurting. He could choose to set aside time, at the end of the day, to be with his thoughts and painful feelings so they wouldn't lead to other dilemmas in his life, such as failing a class or missing out on the pleasures of learning that seemed so much a part of who he was. John said that he would try.

An important piece here is that John understood the reason behind his feelings. He wasn't confused, but really very clear about his feelings. He saw how they were picking up power by intruding into other aspects of his life, and he ultimately made a choice not to deny them, but to really try to manage them.

Not more than a few weeks later, after Spring break, John presented himself in class like his original self. He had, indeed, moved on himself. He had begun dating and was seeing someone else. I suggested that he be mindful of his experience. The knowledge that he had the capacity to bounce back would be an important tool for him to call upon in the future. It would serve as an important part of his self-awareness and capacity to self-soothe.

Consider This: Write about two emotions you know you often experience, and an event that is likely to cause each. If it helps, think about these in relation to your life in school, either about your involvement with other people or regarding your school work.

2. **You can discuss and describe how you feel, rather than act out.**

Let's consider another scenario.

Say you walk into sociology class thirty minutes late. Your professor thinks he's being funny, suggesting that you often party hardy, way too long and too often. Several students join in on the laughter. The truth is that you were up quite late, consoling a friend back home about the death of his parent. You feel angry and embarrassed by your professor's comments, and consider them unprofessional. You feel like telling your professor off, and even dropping the class. How rude he was.

But you take a few moments for yourself. After class you seek out your professor before he leaves. You explain how embarrassing his comments were to you and how uncomfortable you felt. You don't like having attention drawn to you, especially in a negative way. And especially when the comments were unfounded. You were hurt as well, because you worked hard to prepare the assignment that was due that day. You share this with your professor, who listens quietly as you explain your feelings. Your professor is truly apologetic. He thanks you for helping him understand and offers you an opportunity to make up portions of the class you missed during another one of his class sections. You are glad you didn't lash out at your prof, and very happy you didn't drop the class. You handled things well, with good self-awareness. You considered, named, and expressed your feelings.

Sometimes students do the opposite. They "act out." They respond, often in a way that is not helpful to the situation. They overreact, reflecting a feeling or emotion they are experiencing, but not expressing or talking about. When this happens, often times the person is not even aware of what they are really feeling because they haven't taken the time to consider it. Cursing out the professor would have been acting out. Closing down and refusing to pay attention for the rest of the class would have been acting out. Storming out of the classroom would have been acting out. Dropping the class would have been acting out.

Without self-awareness, there are plenty of situations at school that could lead to acting out. A student may be very disappointed about a failing grade, but rather than expressing that disappointment, lashes out at a professor for not being a good teacher. You might be frustrated that your friend consistently bails out after making a plan with you, but rather than tell them that, you purposely don't show up for a lunch date you made with him.

Being self-aware often implies taking a moment, or several, to stop, reflect, and really pay attention to you how you are feeling inside. Then, rather than impulsively responding through action, or overreaction, you can slow down and choose to verbalize or explain those feelings or emotions. You use your self-awareness to express yourself and communicate rationally.

Consider This: How good are you at verbalizing your feelings? Do you do so often? Do you act out? How might you move to better letting out your emotions in words?

3. **You have a vocabulary to explain how you feel.**

Language can help move you from an internal state of discomfort to a more positive, modulated state. Just the simple act of becoming aware of your emotions and naming them, communicating your frustrations, sadness, or upset, begins to soothe you and reduce an emotional reaction. [3] It's like you verbally exhale. You "let it out" and express yourself, rather than stay tied up in knots. It often provides some relief to the internal pain you may be experiencing.

I love the scene from the book, and subsequent movie, Ordinary People by Judith Guest. Conrad, the protagonist, has lost his brother in a boating accident. He's not conscious of the degree of guilt he feels for having survived. In a session with his therapist, Dr. Berger, he is reticent, not wanting to speak of his feelings.

Berger laughs. "When's the last time you got really mad?"

He says, carefully, "When it comes, there's always too much of it. I don't know how to handle it."

"Sure, I know," Berger says. "It's a closet full of junk. You open the door and everything falls out."

"No," he says. "There's a guy in the closet. I don't even know him, that's the problem."

"Only way you're ever gonna get to know him," Berger says, "is to let him out now and then. ..."

"Sometimes," he says, "when you let yourself feel, all you feel is lousy."

Berger nods. "Maybe you gotta feel lousy sometime, in order to feel better. A little advice, kiddo, about feeling. Don't think too much about it. And don't expect it always to tickle" [4]

Dr. Berger makes a lot of good points. You don't want the "junk" to pile up, and that means "cleaning out your closet" every once in a while. He also reminds Conrad not to be afraid of uncomfortable feelings. Accepting that these occur to everyone, but that they don't need to last forever, is very consoling.

The general consensus is that women tend to talk about their feelings more easily and more often than do men. This doesn't come as a surprise to most of us. However, what may be surprising is that women are thought to be better able to shake off depression and bounce back from sadness than males.[5] And it is speculated that this is precisely because women tend to have more personal connections and more verbal exchange with friends and family than do men. Sharing difficult emotions, rather than keeping them locked up inside, helps us feel better.[6]

So when someone asks, "How are you feeling?" it's helpful to have a response beyond just "good" or "lousy". The more articulate you can be about your feelings, especially when they are painful, the easier it is for others to understand you and perhaps provide feedback that is helpful to you to adjust your mood.

Consider This: How often do you "clean out your emotional closet?" What could make it easier for you to do? Jot down your response here.

4. **You know how you learn best; you advocate for yourself and manage your studies.**

How do you get the most out of your study time? If you "have no idea" about the best way for you prepare for exams or complete your assignments, you're not alone. But honestly, embarking upon a life in higher education is a good time to develop some insight. This kind of self-knowledge will help you navigate the world of your learning and get "more bang out of our buck" as you devote your precious time to your schoolwork.

You may have an intuitive understanding of your learning preferences from your experiences in school over the years. Have you considered the circumstances in which you do best? Do you know the best time of day for you to study? How long you go before needing a break? Do you learn best by reading material, listening to it, writing about it, or reciting it out loud? These and other questions can help you ultimately structure your studying in a way that is most effective and provides the biggest payoff.

Perhaps you have been through some testing to assess your intellectual potential (IQ) or cognitive profile. Have you been identified as having a learning disability or any another condition that entitles you to accommodations within your classes? If so, you will want to be aware of these, ask for them yourself and perhaps even explain them to your professors. Accommodations include offerings such as extended time when taking examinations, taking exams in a separate location, having exams printed in large type, or even read aloud to you.

Even if you do not have a documented designation that entitles you to accommodations, it's a good idea to let your professor know your classroom or learning preferences. Perhaps you would rather not read aloud in class because it makes you nervous, or that you want to use a laptop in class rather than take notes by hand. Maybe you like to sit close to the front of the room where you can focus best, or prefer to work independently rather than with a partner or in a group. These are requests you may make on your own behalf. Though they may not always be honored, many professors will do their best to help you out.

Knowing what works best for you, and what makes you feel the most comfortable in your learning environment, is part of self-awareness. It also helps to know this information so that you can advocate, or speak out, for some of your needs.

Consider This: Go online and search for a Learning Style or Learning Preference Inventory. Complete one or two of these with which you feel most comfortable. Think about how you can structure your studies to take your style into account.

5. You make better choices for yourself.

Picture yourself at your favorite restaurant. You're out with your friends ordering dinner. How do you know what to select? Ordering your main dish is a decision you make based on many factors: what you like to eat, how hungry you are, how much money you have to spend on dinner, your wish to eat "healthy"-or not, or maybe even when and where you think you will be eating next.

Beyond ordering dinner, some say that our entire lives are, indeed, the results of the decisions we make. In college, you are bombarded with a multitude of choices and thus a multitude of decisions to make. Each decision you make is based on several different criteria. Your satisfaction with those decisions is related to your capacity to choose best for yourself; based on your knowledge of yourself; who you are, what you want, what is good for you, what you enjoy, where you are headed.

<hr>

In Dr. Howard Thurman's Commencement Address at Spelman College several decades past, the theologian implored students to listen for the "sound of the genuine" in themselves. He said....

"There is something in every one of you that waits and listens for the sound of the genuine in yourself. It is the only true guide you will ever have. And if you cannot hear it, you will all of your life spend your days on the ends of strings that somebody else pulls.... Don't be deceived and thrown off by all the noises ....so that you don't hear the sound of the genuine in you, because that is the only true guide that you will ever have, and if you don't have that you don't have a thing...." [7]

It takes a while, and a good deal of intention, to "hear" your own "genuine." Even after you do, sometimes it takes courage to act on behalf of it, especially if it is contrary to what others are doing or ask you to do.

Choices in college are vast and ongoing. They all require you to know yourself well. They range from figuring out when you should begin studying to be well prepared for your psychology midterm exam to deciding for what time to set your alarm, knowing how long you take to get ready, to be on time for your 8 am chemistry class.

Just the single action of registering for classes is entrenched in self-awareness. You consider the subject areas you like or sound interesting to you, the demands of your major, the number of classes you can manage at one time, the best time of day for you to attend class, the teaching style of professors you enjoy most, whether or not you might be in class with your friend, how difficult you perceive a course to be.

Once you begin a semester, you will decide when to buy your textbooks, when you will complete your classwork, how often you will go to the library, what time to go to bed so you can make it to an early class, or whether you should go out the night before an exam. The list goes on and on. You are called upon regularly to be self-aware so that your decisions are good ones...for you.

Consider This: Here is a list of 10 BIG Decisions related to college life that every student needs to make. The answers to these questions can be practical, but are also very personal. There are no rights or wrongs... only what makes sense for you. Having a real sense of yourself and knowing what works best for you will help you make decisions that will be good ones-for you. Think about them. Respond to as many as you can right now. And remember, it's ok to change your mind over time!

10 BIG Decisions for College Life
. . . .

1. Where will I go to school?
2. When and where will I complete my assignments?
3. What classes will I take each semester?
4. Who will be my friends?
5. Will I work while attending college?
6. What extra-curricular activities will I take part in?
7. Will I attend all my classes?
8. How hard and often will I party?
9. How will I prioritize my schoolwork in the context of my social life, family obligations, athletic involvement, employment obligations and distractions?
10. What are my ultimate goals?

The answers to these, and all the questions you confront during your college days, will combine both your knowledge of the possible options and your awareness of yourself.

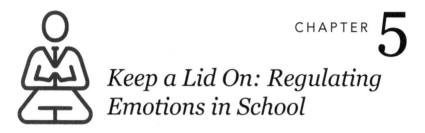

CHAPTER 5

Keep a Lid On: Regulating Emotions in School

"I discovered I always have choices and sometimes it's only a choice of attitude."

— *Judith M. Knowlton, author*

Heading to college is a true milestone in your life, whether you are going away to school or commuting from home. It signals the completion of those early "childhood" school days and transition to a more adult, independent way of living. It marks the beginning of a new chapter in your life.

You'll experience many new "firsts" in college. Educationally, it offers you far more academic choices than high school. Once you move through your required courses, you will be amazed at the number of exciting classes that you can elect to take, across many areas of study. There will probably be classes on subjects you may never even have heard of. You can also begin taking courses that specialize in your areas of interest or future career.

But the college experience goes far beyond what you learn in the classroom. For lots of people, the most exciting aspects of college life occur outside of class. There are clubs and organizations in which to take part, and presentations, fairs, celebrations, political rallies, concerts and sporting events to attend. You can join athletic teams, volunteer groups, musical/theater/dance productions and art workshops. So many wonderful options! College is about socializing, getting involved, making new friends, doing what you love, and having some really great times. It's funny, but if you ask graduates to talk about their college years, most remember all the "wild and crazy" fun and exciting experiences, and not so much about the coursework!

Throughout it all, attending college offers a new level of independence. No one is "standing guard" telling you what to do and how to do it. You select your own courses, plan your own study times, and pick and choose your social activities all on your own. This can feel glorious. Ah... freedom!

Yet, terrific as college life is, traveling into unchartered territory without someone right there to guide and protect you can be challenging and even a little scary.

Once the semester begins, lots of students are surprised, and a bit concerned, about the academic rigors of their courses. I've actually seen panic in the eyes of some students when I distribute the course outline on the first day of class. The outline details the topics we will study during the semester, books to purchase and read, the assignments and projects that are required with their due dates, and the dates of quizzes and exams. While knowing all this in advance helps to plan and manage one's life - and is entirely doable - seeing it all at once can feel like a building crashing down on top of you. If you are taking four or five classes, you can imagine the pressure.

Ironically, all those great non-academic opportunities and activities present some complicated challenges. They can certainly distract you from your studies and take up a lot of time. You will need to monitor this.

Indeed, your new independence comes with new responsibility to make wise and safe decisions. You will need to structure your days and manage your schedule. You might need to deal with adversity, resolve conflicts, advocate on your own behalf, and know when and how to seek help. This is true for academic demands as well as your social interactions.

Let's talk about all this. Your capacity to manage college life, and your related emotions, will serve you well as you navigate your college world. Your ability to tolerate and manage feelings will help you deal with stress and combat its potential power to overwhelm you. This will help you to stay on task, focus, think, and produce! [1]

Acknowledging that challenges and dilemmas are likely to be part of the experience will help you prepare for and manage the feelings that they bring. Hold on to your hats! The experience can be bumpy. But you have strengths and the ability to see yourself through.

The Ups and the Downs of It

Let's walk through some scenarios in which you could very well find yourself during college. They will likely challenge your capacity to resolve a problem, manage and cope. I share them not to concern you, but so you can realize in advance that they are common. They won't just happen to you. They come with the territory. Let's put them out there up front, take away their power, and think about ways to steer the emotional roller coaster of college.

- Simply the number of classes, assignments and exams you are attempting to manage in a single semester may feel overwhelming and stressful. You are determined to succeed in all of your courses, but the amount of work to complete leaves you feeling like you are over the top.

- Your experience in just one class can have you feeling like a bouncing ball of emotions. Let's say you are elated that your psychology professor is the most inspiring teacher you've ever encountered. You are totally into the class. You feel really proud when the professor comments that your participation in classroom discussions is insightful and intelligent. He loves your questions too. You really enjoy being in this class.

   However, you find yourself extremely anxious the night before the first exam and are unable to sleep. Not only that, you worked really hard on a ten page paper about the interpretations of dreams and are blown away, and angry at your wonderful professor, because it came back with a grade of D+. How can a single class trigger such different reactions?

- Other disappointments are possible. How does it feel when you don't make the team or aren't selected as the editor of the school paper, or feel ostracized from a study group, or fail an exam, or ask a question that you feel was "stupid" the second it came out of your mouth? Oh my!

- If you are living on campus and are away from home for the first time, perhaps you miss your family and are even a bit frightened being on your own.

You might feel insecure about reaching out to new friends or are uneasy about living with others you do not know well. Perhaps the lack of privacy in a dorm makes you feel uncomfortable.

- You want to go out for the evening but have so many assignments. How can you tell your friend you don't want to party because you want to study, without feeling like a nerd, or being afraid you will not be included at the next social gathering?

- On a commuter campus there are other social and emotional challenges. It's tough to make friends when everyone is coming and going at different hours. Maybe you are working while going to school and your life feels like a whirlwind. You walk around exhausted and are worried about just finding the time to do any of the assignments. You might feel isolated even though there are so many people around you. How awkward is it to walk into the dining hall and eat by yourself?

These scenarios, problemaic as they appear, are not meant to alarm you. They're to let you know that whatever you are feeling and going through happens to many students...all the time. Though you are unique, many of your concerns and dilemmas are common and shared by others. You are not alone or ever the only person experiencing emotional challenges or an uncomfortable situation. Hold on to that thought whenever you feel like you are. Be mindful that your stresses and discomforts are normal. They will pass, and there are definitely actions you can take to help yourself through the difficult times.

Tolerating and Managing Your Feelings: The Good, the Bad, the Ugly

Remember Dr. Berger's advice to Conrad in Chapter 4. It's important to deal with your emotions so that they don't come crashing down on your head one day. Feelings can be unsettling. This sounds simple, or even obvious, but it is important to keep it in mind. Sometimes things don't go as we had planned, hoped, or expected. That is normal and part of life. It is important that you find your way through these times so that you can get right back on track, focus on your goals, and persevere.

Managing your emotions and regulating your mood is an important capacity for you to develop throughout your college years. It will help you stop stressors from overtaking you, enable you to tolerate frustrations and disappointments, and access that "second wind" to start up again.

We will talk further about this in the context of delaying gratification, in Chapter 7.

Turn Your Back on Dangerous Coping Methods

People cope in different ways. Your objective is to pick out healthy coping strategies, not dangerous ones. This means monitoring the choices you make, perhaps impulsive, that get in the way of achieving your goals. In the worst case scenario, they can be self-destructive. Here are some of those "solutions" college students have been known to apply to deal with difficulties or stress in school. But ultimately, they won't serve your better interest. Watch out for them. Try hard to stay away from them.

- Throwing in the towel and simply giving up can sometimes seem very alluring. It puts an end to the pain. The struggle and the stress is over. Giving up happens in different forms. This can be not attending classes, not completing assignments, dropping classes, or even deciding to leave school. However, the capacity to stay goal directed and not allow yourself to give in to feelings of quitting is significant. It speaks to

your ability to regulate your emotions and persist in the pursuit of your goals, despite difficulty or adversity. This can be the factor that leads
to success that otherwise might pass you by.

This is not to say that changing direction or lessening
the load is wrong. In fact, that intervention may very
well make good and healthy sense, especially when
it enables you to continue on your pathway to achieve
your goals. But be mindful of drastic changes or behaviors that lead to the abandonment of dreams that are
important and meaningful to you.

- Unfortunately, it's very easy to self-medicate
  and numb upsetting feelings with substances
  that can really harm you. They may seem like
  quick fixes to feel better or relax, but they don't
  provide meaningful solutions. You don't want to
  get loaded on alcohol or high on drugs to mask
  uncomfortable or stressful feelings in school.

Should you find yourself doing so, be wise and speak
with a counselor on campus who could help you step
away from that choice and provide you with alternative
ways to cope and relax.

- You also don't want to withdraw or act out.
  If your professor upsets you, it's not a good

idea to tell him or her off or get into a shouting match. Storming out of the classroom in a huff will not serve your better interests.

- Clamming up and holding everything in is not a good idea either. Though it might be your style, and even seem noble and strong of you to not share your feelings, as we've discussed, it's not.

So what should you do when life at school feels overwhelming and you are really stressed out? You **will** want to develop healthy, positive, productive ways to soothe yourself when you run into problems. Let's look more deeply at strategies you can try to regulate your emotions on campus.

Two Ways to Cope

Consider two general ways to manage your stress, identified by researchers Lazarus and Folkman. One is called "*problem-focused coping*" and the other is "*emotion-focused coping*." [2]

Problem-Focused Coping
When you use problem-focused coping, you try to create a practical solution to address what is stressing you out.

For example, let's say you are anxious every morning because you struggle to find a place to park. Your first class doesn't start until 10 am and all the parking spots are taken by the time you get to campus. You might decide to arrive to campus at 9 am, when parking is easier. You could use the extra hour there to study.

Or perhaps you are worried that you are falling behind in your assigned readings because you don't have enough money just yet to pay for your textbooks. You might solve the problem by sharing books with a friend, taking the book out of the college library, (required texts are often on reserve) or finding an online version of the text. Considering a simple solution to an ongoing problem is always a good idea.

Emotion-Focused Coping

When there doesn't seem to be a practical solution to your stress, then you might try emotion-focused coping. Here you attempt to reframe or reduce your negative emotional response to a stressor that just can't be changed.

For example, if a progress report you receive from your professor says you are in jeopardy of failing a class, rather than freak out, you could consider the message a wakeup call. It could motivate you to consult with your professor about how to approach your work more effectively. You could actually thank her for letting you know you were in trouble!

Say you are feeling jittery about an upcoming exam, even though you have studied and know the material very well. You might decide that your anxiety isn't helpful or even warranted, and distract yourself with an evening out rather than stay in and ruminate about the test. Just don't get to bed very late!

If you find yourself alone one evening when everyone else seems to be out, rather than wonder why you weren't included in the plans, you could decide to use the evening as an opportunity to catch up on work, read, text, or just relax and watch TV.

Talking with friends to "let off steam" and vent may not change a situation, but often provides calming relief and can help soothe any situation. It can also bring you closer to others and help forge your relationship with them. Sharing with those you trust is another way to "clean out the closet" rather than let stressful feelings bottle up inside of you.

Whether you use problem-focused coping or emotion-focused coping, the point is to cope! Think of this as adapting to a situation, rather than collapsing. Having the ability to adapt is an important social and emotional competency. It may very well enable you to persist when others give up.

More Ideas for Holding it Together
• •

Here are some other suggestions that you might consider when you are feeling emotionally frazzled.

Physical activity can help alleviate stress. Working out, taking a walk, swimming, biking, dancing, or playing any kind of sport relieves muscle tension and gets those endorphins pumping to help you feel better. Doing yoga or ti chi can do the same. You might include physical education classes in your schedule for credit towards elective requirements, even if phys ed is not your major! Colleges often have well equipped gym areas and exercise classes available to students outside of coursework. Find out what your school offers and take advantage of a "free" gym membership.

On the flip side, many students have found meditation an effective way to calm a frenetic mind to find relaxation and peace. See if your school provides any of these opportunities.

Get involved in something you like. This not only helps take your mind off your concerns, but brings joy into your life. That's why extra-curricular activities are not only good for your future resumé, but good for your spirits and soul. Engage! Often the busier you are, in a variety of different activities, the happier you are. If you enjoy it....then do it!

Don't be concerned with how "good" you are if you are having fun. Sing loud, play the trombone, sign up for a dance troupe, hit that baseball, paint a picture, photograph a sunset, create a new recipe, groom a puppy, write a poem, join an improvisation group, design a necklace......**DO WHATEVER FLOATS YOUR BOAT!**

College is your time to explore and enrich your life. I'm amazed at the number of clubs that exist on some campuses that provide something for everyone. Check out your school's offerings, or do what you love on your own or with friends.

Eat well! Being hydrated and eating healthy food has an impact on your emotional as well as physical health. [3] Drink plenty of water. Try to maintain a balanced diet that includes adequate amounts of fruit, vegetables, dairy, protein and grains. Limit your intake of sugars, salt, and alcohol. Sometimes it's a challenge to eat the right kinds of food at college, especially if you are eating on the run or not inclined to cook for yourself. Campuses are working harder to offer healthy food choices. Go with healthy! You can learn more about what really constitutes a healthy diet by going to the US Department of Agriculture website, MyPlate.gov. [4]

Talk with your professors. If you are feeling confused or uncomfortable about anything related to your classroom experience, you may be surprised how connecting with your professor can help. Professors are usually caring, approachable people and can be a source of comfort and guidance for you. Most professors have office hours in their schedule, during which time they are available to students. Take a chance and reach out to a professor to discuss any questions or concerns you may have.

Get Counseling. There may be times when you are really overwhelmed, isolated, or just feeling unhappy. As we said, going away to college may be the first time you are unsupervised or away from your family and close friends. Even if you are living at home and commuting to school, you are on your own more so than ever before, with new demands and expectations. While the freedom is enticing, it can also feel lonely, detached, and downright scary. If you are feeling that way, or unable to resolve issues that are troubling you, it makes good sense to **contact a counselor on campus and get some help**. It may only be one meeting or a series of appointments. Every institution has an office or center for psychological counseling and support. Take advantage of this offering. The reason these services exist is that it is understood that they are needed. The contacts are confidential. There is absolutely nothing to be embarrassed about when it comes to seeking this kind of support. In fact, it is wise. Sharing your concerns and being open to getting input that can help you is an emotionally intelligent thing to do.

Being able to regulate your moods and help yourself through difficult emotional times is vital for your wellbeing and peace of mind. Beyond that, managing your emotions enables you to work through conflict and pain in relationships. It helps you persevere when you may feel like giving up. It enables you to renew your commitment and efforts in pursuit of your goals. For sure, it has a huge impact on the quality and outcomes of your college life. And that is just what we will discuss in depth in the next chapter.

A Word About Optimism

"A pessimist sees the difficulty in every opportunity; an optimist sees the opportunity in every difficulty."

— *Winston Churchill, former British Prime Minister*

To the extent that you can be optimistic, no matter how difficult or stressful times may be, the better you will do and feel. Optimism is the capacity to be hopeful and have confidence about the future or the successful outcome of something. It is the belief that things can turn out alright, or even great, despite the difficulties or dilemmas you may need to go through to get to the other side. Psychologist Martin Seligman teaches us that if we can explain life to ourselves in a positive way and with hope, rather than see difficulties as all-encompassing and never ending, we can move past challenges with greater ease. And optimism leads to success. Seligman wrote, "A composer can have all the talent of Mozart and a passionate desire to succeed, but if he believes he cannot compose music, he will come to nothing. He will not try hard enough. He will give up too soon when the elusive right melody takes too long to materialize." [5]

So try to stay positive. Surround yourself with friends and mentors who are upbeat and hopeful. They inherently understand that the sun will shine after the rain. It always does. And when it rains again...as it will... the sun will come out. The essence of the song, "Tomorrow," from the musical show *Annie*, is all about that. The sun *will* come out ....and it's only "a day away."

Consider This: Take a moment to think about how you may have already used a problem-focused strategy and an emotion- focused strategy to cope with a challenging situation. Write about them here.

CHAPTER **6**

Reach for the Stars: Setting Your Goals

"Reach high, for stars lie hidden in you. Dream deep, for every dream precedes the goal."

— *Rabindranath Tagore, 19th Century Bengali writer, musician, and artist*

"Obstacles are things a person sees when he takes his eyes off his goal."

— *E. Joseph Cossman, author and entrepreneur*

In a legendary Broadway musical called *South Pacific*, a lead character sings a song called "Happy Talk." Part of the chorus goes like this:

Happy Talk, keep talkin Happy Talk
Talk about things you like to do.
You got to have a dream

If you don't have a dream
How you gonna have a dream come true?

— Rogers and Hammerstein, 1949[1]

So much about college is having a dream. Dreams can morph into your goals. They reflect your hopes, desires, vision for the future and maybe even your fantasies. However you name them, having personal goals is an important aspect of being socially and emotionally strong.

Goals provide direction as you carve out your pathway to reach them. Studies have shown that students who can articulate their goals actually achieve better than those who say that they have no idea what they would want to do in the future.[2] Those who have the ability to set and identify realistic, meaningful targets for themselves have a far greater chance of reaching their objectives than those who don't.[3]

This doesn't mean that you must know exactly what you want to "be" or "do" after graduation at the time you start college. Many students don't even decide on a major before the end of their junior year. They use the early years of college to explore different areas of study, options and interests to see what's out there. You may pursue several different paths in your college life, based on your interests, curiosities, and talent. But to the extent that you consciously try to crystalize your focus and hone in on an objective that integrates your abilities, knowledge and your preferences, the more likely you will be able to persevere, reach your stars, and realize your dreams.

Grit Matters

No matter what your dream, researchers suggest that all successful achievers and prominent leaders in any walk of life share a particular personality trait. It is called grit. Grit refers to perseverance and passion put to work towards a long-term goal. People with grit have the capacity to work strenuously through challenges and maintain effort and interest, even despite hard times, failure and obstacles.[4] While others might succumb to disappointment or boredom and change their course of focus, the person with grit has the stamina to stay the course and pursue the dream, and achieve success.

Grit is a great quality, and it often separates those who achieve from those who just come close. Think about those things in your life that you never give up on. They may indicate the grit in you.

Three O's of Goal Setting

Related to grit, three important concepts really help you create and reach meaningful goals while you are in college. I think of these as the Three O's of Goal Setting: Ownership, Optimism, and Opportunity.

Ownership

You are the master of your own journey through college. Although counselors may provide advice, professors will set course objectives, and family and friends may influence you, the overriding choices about where you are headed and how you will get there are yours. Internalize your goals. Make them a part of you. *Set goals for yourself, not only about where you are headed, but about the quality of your performance as you work towards getting there.*

Be autonomous about the goals you make. This means that you take ownership of your goals. This will help motivate you to reach them. Where do **you** want to go? How do **you** intend to get there? What do **you** want each step to look like? Considering these questions - in advance of your actions - creates *intentionality.* You state what you *intend* to accomplish. You make it real. You orchestrate your path and take charge. This can be from the smallest step (*I won't go out tonight. I'll read Chapter 8 and have my summary written by Tuesday morning*) to the bigger picture *(I will earn my B.S. degree in Business Administration in four years, work in a patent office upon graduation, save some money and start law school focusing on intellectual property the following year.)* Wow!

Don't feel frightened to set a specific goal. You can always change your mind! Seriously, that's ok. It's all part of a process. Adjusting and rebooting is a sign of thoughtfulness, realism, and growth. But at the same time, remember grit; that the capacity to stick to your dream, and not waiver off your intended objective or get thrown off by fear, concern, or doubt, is a quality that you will do well to nurture and try hard to live by.

Optimism
The ability to marshal your energy and efforts in pursuit of your goals is tremendously strengthened by your level of optimism. Simply stated, optimism is your capacity to be hopeful. As Vince Lombardi, the great

football player and coach, once said, "We would accomplish many more things if we did not think of them as impossible."

It's true. *Researchers reveal that believing in oneself, having real faith in your ability to achieve success and attain a positive outcome, is a pivotal factor in achieving that success.* [5] This might require some conscious effort. As mentioned in Chapter 5, optimism, the capacity to be positive and hopeful about the future, is a personality trait that develops in us over our lives. But, as psychologist Dr. Martin Seligman shares, we can consciously *learn* to think positively and be optimistic. [6] Intending to be hopeful and behaving in a positive, confident way, fosters a more optimistic mindset, even if it isn't there to start. We can adjust how we explain, understand, and manage adversity or failures in our lives.

So no matter what disappointments you may have experienced in the past, try to let your college experience be, as the poster said, the first day of the rest of your life. Approach it, your classes, assignments, relationships, and your goals, with hope and a sense that you will be successful. I'd recommend that you take a look at Dr. Seligman's book, *Learned Optimism: How to Change Your Mind and Your Life.*

Opportunity

Many people attribute getting ahead to being in the right place at the right time. Perhaps this is a form of being lucky. Going to college is, in fact, a form of being in the right place at the right time. For all of the years you spend in higher education, you have a special opportunity to check out life's possibilities and chart your pathway to objectives that intrigue, stimulate, or resonate with you. *Attending college is a unique time in your life to consider your goals and your future.*

Seize the moments of your college years to explore and refine your goals. Embrace the the many personal resources around you to help. Meet with educational and vocational counselors on campus to learn of career and vocational options and trends in the job market. These professionals can help you to identify and shape your career goals. Consult with your family about your aspirations. Connect with your professors to help establish attainable goals for yourself in every class you take. Talk with your friends about their goals as you reflect upon your own. Always work hard in the steps you take to reach the goals you set.

Whatever goals you set for yourself, latch onto them with gusto. Believe that you can accomplish anything that you set your mind to. Oftentimes, that's what it takes to get there.

The Long and the Short of It...and Somewhere In Between

While you are in school, consider your **short term, long term and intermediate goals**.

Long term goals encompass relatively longer periods of time, perhaps from one to five years. Your long term goal might include the kind of degree you want to attain, when you would like to get it, and the career path you plan to pursue upon graduation.

Intermediate goals embody the steps you need to take along the way to accomplish that longer term objective. Say your long term goal is to obtain your nursing degree and work as a pediatric nurse in a hospital in New York City. An intermediate goal could include fulfilling all the prerequisites to apply to a nursing program and to attain an associate's degree before moving on to the four year program. You would then intend to pass the requisite licensing exam (another intermediate goal), apply to four hospitals (again another intermediary goal) and finally accept a position.

Short term goals cover the least amount of time. In college, they can include your daily objectives, like generating a "to do" list for yourself every day, ie. "I will attend all of my classes today. Later, between the hours of 3 and 7 pm, I will complete any assignments that are due tomorrow." Your short term goals might reflect your commitment to turn in all assignments on time in a given semester, and to attain grades of B or better on projects, exams and final grades in all of your courses.

Sometimes it helps to organize your thinking by identifying your long term goal first. Then you can back track and consider the intermediate steps you need to achieve along the way to get there. Finally, look at the short term goals embodied in each of the intermediate steps.

Tips for Establishing Meaningful Goals

Here are some additional tips for setting your goals in school.

1. **Be real! Create realistic, doable goals that push you to succeed.**

It can be a bit tricky, but the more specific you can be in stating your goals, the more meaningful and measureable they become. Notice the difference between the three statements that follow about a student's goals for grades in a given semester:

I just want to pass my classes.

I want to do well in all my classes

I will work to get an A in my psychology and history class, at least a B+ in English, and C+ or better in math and science.

All of the statements do indicate a goal for the semester. The first is the least challenging, without any drive to do quality work or differentiate among the classes. The second is more positive, but is still a generic statement without any bar setting or statement of achievement objectives. The final statement sets real, specific, personal expectations, as well as standards by which the student can measure whether or not she has met her goals. The goals reflect the student's awareness of her academic strengths and weaknesses and adjust expectations based on that knowledge.

Here's a really important point. Adding a "***by***" clause forces you to be thoughtful about the goals you set. It helps you identify *how* you will accomplish them. For example, "*I will work to get an A in my psychology class **by** ... never missing a class, reviewing and highlighting my notes after class, assigning myself textbook portions to read on a nightly basis, studying for exams at least three days in advance of the test, and meeting with my professor at least twice during the semester to review my progress.*" WHEW...that's setting a goal and telling it like it is!

You may set goals for yourself in other venues related to college life. Perhaps you have a desire to be more social and develop friendships, to get more organized and manage your time better, to be more focused in classes, or to take part in extra-curricular activities. These are all legitimate areas for goal setting. Think about how you could establish your own personal goals to succeed in these areas.

2. The pen is mighty! Write down your goals.

This is the "pedal to the metal" part of setting goals. When you actually articulate your goals in writing, you force yourself to clarify your intentions. Goals take on new meaning and power when you say them, and when you state them in writing they really come alive. It also records your intentions to which you can return periodically to check on and monitor.

3. Consider your guideposts: Be mindful of your goals.

Let your goals be your conscience. Keep them in mind to pull yourself back in when you might be enticed to stray or go off track. For example, didn't you say you were aiming for an A in psychology this semester? So call upon that goal when your friend asks you to go out with her the night before the exam. Be true to your goal, and stay home, study, and rest.

Typically as a college student, no one is standing over you to manage your behavior. You need to manage your self. (We'll discuss this in depth in the next chapter.) One strategy to help you here is to recall the objectives you have set for yourself, and allow those intentions to modify how you behave....Hopefully for the better!

4. Reboot! It's ok to change your mind.

Give yourself permission to revise your goals as you move along. Review your goals periodically and see if they are still appropriate. Yes, not giving up on your objectives is an important social and emotional quality. BUT, college is a time of exploration and learning, and you may discover new opportunities or ideas along the way that compel you to reconsider. Or you may just need to adjust aspects of your goals because of logistics or practical issues.

Perhaps at the beginning of the semester you targeted a C+ in your African American Literature class. Once the course begins, you find yourself enjoying the readings and doing well with the written assignments. Your professor is supportive and praises your comments in class discussions. You earn a 97 on the first quiz and an A- on your first literary response. Maybe this is a good time to adjust your goal to achieving at least a B+ or even an A in the class, and work hard to maintain your success.

You may need to revise your goals to accommodate changes in your life situation. As they say, "Life gets in the way." Sometimes we just need to bow to outside circumstances. For instance, though your intention may have been to complete your bachelor's degree in four years, you might need to take a semester off to care for an ailing relative or even your own health issues. Or perhaps you find that you can only manage the coursework in three or four classes each semester, rather than the five needed to complete your degree in four years. Or maybe you need to work 35 hours a week at your job and simply don't have the time. Five classes are just too much. In those cases, you would need to adjust one aspect of your goal, that is, how long it will take you to attain it, without throwing away the goal altogether. The focus is still the degree - to which you are very much committed - and you wisely give yourself permission to accomplish it in five years, rather than four.

At these times it's important to keep your eyes on the bigger prize and not allow circumstances or obstacles derail you altogether. Be gritty! Your goals are still very much attainable, albeit they may take a little longer time in coming. A degree earned in five years works as well one earned in four. As I often tell my students when this occurs, "OK...you'll just be out there in the workplace for 49 years, not 50!" Ugh!

Go for the Gold!

Hockey legend Wayne Gretsky famously quipped, "You miss 100% of the shots you don't take." Keep that in mind when you may be feeling less than positive about taking a chance or stepping forward to try. We all have our doubts and our moments of insecurities. But, as another famous line reminds us, "You've got to be in it to win it." Try to set your standards high, always do your best work, get help when you need it, and take those chances to reach the dreams you dream.

Consider This: Take a moment to write down at least one short term, long-term and intermediate goal you have for yourself right now. Try to add a *by* clause for each. Good luck!

A short term goal:

An intermediate goal:

A long term goal:

CHAPTER 7

Stay on Top of It: Strategies for Self-Monitoring

"I am thankful to all those who said 'No' to me. It is because of them that I am doing it myself."

— Albert Einstein, theoretical physicist

Here's some good news and some bad news about college. The good news is that no one is standing over you, keeping track of how you are doing. The bad news is that no one is standing over you, keeping track of how you are doing!

You are now the master of your own destiny. When you enroll as a college student, the college has a contract with you; not your parents, spouse, family member, or counselor. In fact, college personnel, including your professors, deans, and advisors, need *your* permission to discuss any matters concerning you. These include your grades, conduct, and finances. That's very empowering, isn't it? However, this new reality creates a high level of responsibility for you. The truth is that YOU are in charge of your college life. You are your own director, guardian, and guidance counselor.

This shift to self-ownership and responsibility for your life embraces an important element of social and emotional intelligence. It is the capacity to self-monitor. Self-monitoring relates directly to your academic, as well as personal success in school.

Self-monitoring is the ability to track and evaluate your own performance. In essence, you ask yourself, "How am I doing?" This is across a variety of scenarios; within your coursework and all of your personal endeavors outside of class. You want to be able to respond honestly and accurately. Researchers have discovered that taking the time to regularly self-monitor, seriously and thoughtfully, can lead to positive changes in your performance. It increases your self-awareness and forces you to pay attention to your behavior. [1]

Self-monitoring not only asks you to know how you are doing, but what you are doing! It puts your academic focus into a context. For example, can you identify the unit of study you just completed in math...or history or whatever subjects you are taking? What was the last topic you learned about? What were the critical points?

Where does that fit into the entire course syllabus? What will you be studying next?

When a student exclaims, "Gee... I have no idea what we are studying in Introduction to Criminal Justice," or whatever the subject might be, that's not a good sign. You want to be connected with your courses and in control of your studying and learning process.

You also want to be conscious of your academic pathway. What classes do you anticipate taking each year? How will these lead you to your scholarly goals? You want to know the answers to these questions and be at the top of your game in college.

Several actions related to self-monitoring are significant for triumphing in college. Some relate to your general approach and planning of your college life and others reflect how you oversee your academic responsibilities; your approach to classes and course work and assignments, both in and out of class. Let's check out these important behaviors.

Call Out Your Intentions

As in goal setting, an important underpinning of self-monitoring is the concept of *intentionality*. In college it really helps to be aware of what you want to accomplish every day and every time you sit down to study.

As a behavior, this means identifying what you *intend* to achieve through your actions....as specifically as you can. Say it out loud, or even write it down.

For example, when you settle in to study for your first exam in environmental science, state what you intend to accomplish. Identify the pages you will cover, the concepts you will review, and what you will be able to do, say, explain, or discuss by the time you are finished. "I'm going to look over environmental science tonight," is a very nebulous, vague objective. It doesn't hold you accountable in any way that you can measure when you finish.

Instead, voice your *specific* intention. You might say, *"I will re-read and annotate Section 1-1 from the first chapter of my Environmental Science text. When I'm finished, I will identify and then explain the seven major environmental conditions that challenge our planet today."* You will be able to judge your success by whether or not you have met your intention. Stating your intentions in a specific way also reveals your real connection to the material.

Creating your intentions is like an affirmation. It turns a general or vague concept into a concrete, conscious action plan that helps motivate yourself. You can refer back to it to measure and monitor your performance.

Another good way to monitor yourself on a daily basis is to establish a "To Do" list. Write a list of what you intend to take care of every day. Track your progress by checking off items as you complete them.

To Do List   Date: _____

Check When Completed	Task	Deadline
☆	_____	
☆	_____	
☆	_____	
☐	_____	
☐	_____	
☐	_____	
☐	_____	
☐	_____	
☐	_____	
☐	_____	
☐	_____	
☐	_____	

You might incorporate your To Do List with your daily planner, which we will discuss in a while. It may help you to see it next to your daily schedule.

You could even create a list for every class you are taking so that you are on top of all of your assignments.

Prioritize your list to call out the most important tasks with a star or underline. It's very satisfying to check off the items as they are completed, or at the end of each day. Those that you didn't get to can be moved onto the next day's agenda. Set limits for yourself. If an important item continues not to get a check, say for three days in a row, then you need to make sure it gets done before anything else on the following day. It would be important to consider why this important task isn't getting done. Are you procrastinating for some reason? (We'll discuss procrastination soon....no pun intended!) Or do you just run out of time?!

Manage Your Time!

Managing time while in college is a major challenge for students. Yet, the ability to manage their time may well be the most important factor leading to success in school. It will definitely help you triumph.

Every year, at institutions from community colleges to Ivy League universities, students fail out. Often, this is not because they are unable to comprehend their subjects or that they lack the skills to complete the work. They just don't give themselves enough time to do it. Students don't hand in assignments when they are due. They don't leave appropriate amounts of study time to prepare for exams.

They often submit work at a level far beneath their own potential or the standards of the class because they didn't allocate enough time to plan, compose, edit and tweak their creation. Quality work takes time, effort and revision.

Compared to high school your time spent in classes is minimal. The average high school student spends about 30 hours in class each week. College students spend about half that time. You may have a class only once or twice a week. Generally, that seems great when you first register for classes. Unfortunately, that's where part of the problem lies. Students perceive that they have "so much free time." That is usually far from the truth.

The reality is that you need to allocate a tremendous amount of time, every day and every week, to study and complete the projects, assignments and readings that are part of the class requirements. This is a very rude awakening for many first year students.

It is recommended that college students allot two hours of study time for each contact hour of classes to successfully manage the content of the class. So, for 15 hours of contact time in the classroom weekly, (three hours a day, five days a week) this adds up to 30 *additional* hours of independent study. [2] Of course this may vary depending upon how efficient you are in completing your work, and the demands of a particular class. The point is that you need to regularly devote time each day to address your assignments and prepare for exams.

Lots of students don't do this. They think that when classes are finished, they are done for the day. Unfortunately, these students are setting themselves up for failure. Pleeeeeease believe me.

But also believe that devoting enough time to address all of your coursework is entirely doable! Let's look at several strategies that you can put into place to successfully manage your time in school. They are all within your power to use. Consider them seriously.

• *Assign Yourself*

Make it your business to *assign yourself* blocks of time in your weekly schedule - in addition to your time in classes - to study, go to the library, and get your work done. Remember the recommendation of two hours of study time weekly for every hour you are in class, for each course! That really adds up to a lot of time and it is! It will create a fuller workweek devoted to your academics. Building time into your weekly schedule to 'take care of business' will impact the quality of your achievements and scholarly mindset.

You might find that you don't need all that time, or you may discover that you need to allocate more. Some classes are very demanding of time, especially those in the sciences. They typically include unfamiliar or technical content and additional lab requirements. *Whatever the case, begin your college experience knowing that your school work will take up a lot of your time; probably more than you thought. You want to succeed, so allocate the time you need to do great work. Be honest. Make it a priority.*

- ***Build a Workable Schedule…Stay on Campus***

When registering for classes, don't feel you need to make them all back to back, or squeeze them into a short period of time within the day so you can be "off" the rest of the day. Use the time you have *between* classes to keep you in the "scholarly" mode of being on campus and tending to your studies. Many students accomplish more by staying on campus, rather than leaving for home or the dorm the minute their last class is completed, or when they have a break. Use those gaps between classes, or time directly before or after them, to eat, get some work done, go to the library, engage in an extracurricular activities, meet with a professor, seek extra help, or just relax if you need to.

Really consider staying on campus beyond your scheduled class time. It can afford you an environment that may be more conducive for you to study or complete assignments rather than at home, your apartment, the dorm, or frat house. Start thinking of that additional time as part of your day at school. The library, designated quiet areas on campus, learning labs, or even a professor's office, may provide the perfect spot for you to get work done or study. Often there is someone available to help you or answer your questions. Take advantage of those spaces. Leave campus a little bit later.

- ***Use a Planner***

I encourage my students to be closet nerds. Just like most business executives do, keep a calendar. Use a planner. Note the times you are in class, and designate all the hours before and after classes that you will use to study and complete your assignments.

Also use your planner to keep track of important dates in your coursework. I strongly recommend a planner in which you can see an entire week at one time. That way you have a sense of what each week will hold, as you approach it.

At the onset of every semester, your professors will distribute or post their course syllabus. For each class, this document identifies the goals or objectives and topics of study for the term. It includes the dates of specific assignments, projects, quizzes, and exams, including midterms and final examinations. *As soon as you have the syllabus of a course you are taking, flip or scroll through the pages in your planner and enter the important due dates noted by each professor.* In this way you will see, in advance, how your academic life will unfold over the next fifteen or sixteen weeks.

Finally, make your planner holistic. Enter all of the other activities or commitments you have in your life. These could include doctor's appointments, club meetings, athletic practice, hours at work, family gatherings, and social activities, like concerts, parties, and dates. This will give you a real graphic depiction of your whole life. And it will help you to schedule your personal commitments around the needs of your academic demands. (Forget about getting concert tickets the night before your final exam!)

• *Don't Be Late*

Both you and your assignments need to be on time!

It's true that "better late than never" is operative when discussing going to classes. It's always the wiser choice to attend class rather than to skip it. But being on time is always better than being late. Walking into class after it has begun can be disruptive to both the other students and to the professor.

Most professors I work with feel very strongly that students arrive to their class on time. The same way you wouldn't be late for your job, an important event, or an interview, so it is for class. Arriving on time is considered not only a responsibility and common courtesy, but a sign of respect for the class and the professor. I know colleagues who are so adamant about this that once class has begun they close the door and students are no longer permitted to enter. Yikes! Get to class on time.

On the other hand, professors are human! They know that life happens and that a person can be unavoidably delayed. You'll find out that professors themselves are sometimes late for their own classes. If you must arrive late to class, it's best to walk into the room quietly and quickly. Take a seat and be as unobtrusive as possible. Perhaps let the professor know at the end of class that you regret your tardiness. Oh…and try not to walk in sipping an iced tea or eating a Big Mac!

Being punctual is important for your own purposes as well. You may miss important introductory content that provides the background knowledge you need to best understand the rest of the lesson. Also, sometimes professors use the first part of class to answer questions, review past material, or make announcements. You don't want to miss this. Finally, walking in late, especially if it is chronic or regular, calls attention to yourself in a negative way. And you don't want that.

If you discover that it is just impossible for you to arrive on time to a particular class because of practical issues, try to make adjustments in your schedule. You may be able to make changes in your school schedule if you are within a designated period of dropping and adding classes. Perhaps a change in your work schedule will accommodate your school schedule. Adjusting your choice of transportation might help. Taking a different bus or train may solve the problem.

You may need to make other modifications related to logistical issues. Perhaps you could get up earlier and arrive to campus further in advance of your class. You can use the wait time to study or complete assignments. This may also help you find parking more readily on campus, as spots are less available as the day progresses. You could ask your professor if he or she teaches another section that you may attend if the timing of that class turns out to work better for you. You might even inform your professor of your dilemma and ask for their suggestions. No matter what, just don't blame your lateness on a faulty alarm clock! Get one that works, or set your phone!

• *Assignments Should Be On Time Too*

Handing assignments in late has a lot in common with being late to class. It works against you. Yes, once again, it's better to hand in an assignment after its due date rather than not at all. But you should strive to do better. Chances are if the work is late, then you didn't manage your time well enough. Your paper or project may be rushed, not reviewed and edited properly, and ultimately, not reflect your best work.

Ironically, if you submit an assignment late because you needed to devote a good amount of time and effort to finish it, you suffer the consequences of a reduced grade for lateness when you actually worked hard and thoroughly! That is a shame. The implication here is that you didn't start soon enough. Back track and afford your assignments the time they need from the beginning, not at the end. You really may be misjudging the amount of time it takes to complete your work well enough to earn a good grade.

The reality is that many students do leave a lot of assignments to the "last minute." If that doesn't work in your better interest, here's a thought....There's nothing wrong with finishing something before the due date! Take your leisure or free time after you complete your work, as your reward. Don't gift it to yourself before you have completed your task.

If lateness is happening because of too much partying the night before, or because there are other places you'd rather be than in class, then a lot of adjustment is in order. And that's all part of effective self-monitoring. Don't beat yourself over the head for messing up...but, do it better next time.

Consider This: Look back over the suggestions for managing your time in college. Which ones do you already do? Which strategies might you try to incorporate into your life in college to be more in control of managing your workload?

CHAPTER **8**

Hold Yourself Accountable:
☆☆✅☆☆ *Self-Monitoring on*
a Deeper Level

W̶ithin other, more internalized levels of self-monitoring, important qualities essential for rising in
college exist. In fact, these capacities impact your success in many areas of your life. Amazingly, they are
often left out of discussions about getting ready for the
college world. So let's meet them now.

Delay Gratification

Along with developing time management tools, your capacity to delay gratification and resist temptation is critical
for success in college. Resisting impulses that lead you
away from your objectives and goals is a key tenet of social and emotional intelligence.[1]

Your capacity to put off fun in order to commit to and complete your studies is MAJOR. Doing so correlates with success in school. Realize that good times can roll, but they may just need to wait a bit.

The power to resist temptation and delay gratification seeps into many aspects of your college existence. You use it to continue writing a paper even when you are exhausted and just want to crash. It helps you keep on studying for exams when there are three parties going on that most of your friends are attending. It has you read your organic chemistry textbook despite the conclusion of your favorite mini-series being on TV. Your ability to delay gratification guides you to finish your senior year even though you might be offered a well-paying job that doesn't require a college degree.

Delaying gratification means you can resist the temptations, impulses and other distractions that could take you off course from your original intentions. This ability is fundamental to staying focused and persisting in anything you do, especially in the face of difficulty or hardship. It means you can carry on, though you might feel like stopping or doing something else.

It's Not How Many Times You Fall Down
Delaying gratification is especially challenging in the face of adversity, hardship, or disappointment. It really is tough to continue working hard in a class when

you have failed the first two quizzes, or gotten a D on the paper on which you spent a tremendous amount of time. You may just want to give up and avoid any further pain. The challenge, then, is to reboot and do what you need to get back on track. Perhaps this means meeting with your professor and getting extra help, talking with an educational counselor, getting tutorial support, changing your study schedule or hours at work, or connecting with a classmate who can help you a bit.

The challenge is to not give into impulses that distract you from your objectives. You will need to incorporate the capacity to delay gratification and resist temptations on many fronts. Let's consider two of the most common challenges in college, as I advise you to show up and unplug!

Show Up

I recently surveyed about 300 professors at the college where I teach. They identified the reasons for student failures in their classes. Poor attendance made everyone's list.[2] Absence always sets you back, even a little, from being on top of the course content and movement of the class. Missing class regularly can be a disaster. As screenwriter Woody Allen asserted, "80% of success is just showing up."

The temptation to cut class in college can be irresistible to some students. It's unlikely that there is a person in your life forcing you to go! Not every professor will even take attendance or consider attendance a component of your grade. Don't be fooled. It **is** a part of your grade, because your understanding of the material, your "knowing what's going on," and your connection to the flow of the class matters a great deal in your management and preparation of your work. Regular attendance keeps you involved and engaged. Even if you don't verbally participate much on a particular day, being there is better than being absent. And frankly, no matter the grading policy, professors do like to see you in their classes.

Early morning classes are particularly rough for students. The temptation to sleep late, especially if you've had a big night out, can be a real challenge. On the flip side, making it to your evening Psychology 203 class when it happens to be on the same night as a nearby concert of your favorite performer is also a bit tricky. Try not to succumb. Go to class!

If you know in advance that you have a conflict with a particular class, see if your professor will allow you to attend a different section of the same class instead. If you just can't help but be absent, be sure to connect with a classmate or the professor to find out what you missed.

Unplug
A 2013 study suggests that college students who are "high-frequency cellphone users" report "higher levels

of anxiety, less satisfaction with life and lower grades than peers who use their cellphones less frequently." This research, taking place at Kent State University, found that on average, students reported spending almost five hours a day using their cellphones, sending nearly 80 messages a day. [3] I would imagine the number of daily messages have sky rocketed since this study first came out.

It's pretty clear that most of us use our cellphones regularly. But texting throughout a class or constantly checking for texts can be a real problem. At its least, staying connected to your phone during class is a distraction. If you are using it regularly, you can end up missing an entire class even while sitting in your seat!

The idea of multi-tasking is a myth. If you are texting, your attention is on the text and not on the lesson. While cellphones are acceptable in some classes, and are even used as instructional devices, for many professors they are an anathema and are prohibited in their classes.

Making a decision to unplug your phone, and other media and technology while you are studying or completing assignments, is admittedly quite tough for a lot of us. It's very difficult to turn away from the seduction of a video game or the desire to be in constant communication and "connected" on a cell phone. Some liken the need to check a cellphone to any other type of addiction. But short of that, you do have a choice. Realize that your productivity, and ultimately the quality of your work is jeopardized if your attention is consistently distracted or interrupted.

As Professor Andre Lepp, author of the Kent State study says, "Students need to shut off their phones, ignore text messages and try to insulate themselves from some of the extraneous distractions that reduce the quality of their work ....and learn how to be alone with yourself." [4]

Being able to turn off your phone for the duration of a class is an example of resisting impulse and delaying gratification. It is a sign of your emotional intelligence. Challenge yourself to do it. You can always catch up when the class is over. Consider your renewed phone use as your reward for having impeded it for a period of time.

Consider This: When you think about yourself, what generally tends to draw you away or distract you from your studies? What could you do to resist the temptation to get side tracked, so that you could complete the task you set out to accomplish?

Break Up with Procrastination
· ·

"Me? A procrastinator? I'll prove you
wrong. Just you wait and see!"

— *Anonymous*

When it comes to a discussion of self-monitoring and college success, we must acknowledge a very deceptive charmer on campus. Perhaps you've met before? Say hello to procrastination.

Of course procrastination is far from a friend. Albeit seductive, it definitely undermines success, not to mention peace of mind, in college. Breaking up with procrastination is the way to triumph! You will need to study and complete assignments throughout all of your college years. You want to be timely and afford enough attention to your work for it to be of high quality. Don't give yourself permission to procrastinate.

Simply stated, you procrastinate when you put off things you should be tending to now, often in favor of doing something more pleasurable or that you are more comfortable doing.[5] In more formal terms, psychologist Clarry Lay explains that procrastination occurs when there is a significant time period between when one intends to take care of something and when they actually do it. [6]

Procrastination rears its head in two basic ways:

delaying or postponing the start of a task or not completing the work on time once you have begun. It's a very familiar ally to those who have a difficult time delaying gratification, because procrastinators are often doing something more enjoyable...anything....rather than their school work.

Some may say that there's a fine line between working well with a deadline and procrastination. We do know that when a professor announces that an assignment is due by the end of the day on April 10, over 95% of the papers will be sent electronically on April 10 at 11:59 pm! So you wouldn't be alone if you waited until the last minute to submit your work.

Let's look at the fine line. **IF** you submit your paper at the last minute because you structured the time you had between getting the assignment and the due date into an action plan, **and** you completed important portions and drafts along the way according to your plan, **and** this included time to review and edit your work so that it was your best, **and** then you submitted it on the due date....then you did well!

IF, however, you submitted the paper at 11:59 pm because you left it until 10:30 pm, **and** the first and only draft was completed at 11:58 and 30 seconds, well, you get the idea. Procrastinators may fool themselves into believing that they work best under pressure, but the truth is, the work that is completed in this way is rarely, if ever, their best. In fact, it usually reveals itself as incomplete, rushed, and full of mistakes.

Managing your time and monitoring your progress, then, counteracts procrastination. Here are a few more points about the procrastination beast that will help you keep it from getting its paws on you!

Why Would You Procrastinate? What Can You Do About It?

People procrastinate for different reasons. Let's consider those of a college student.

I'm so distracted!

There are billions...well, lots of distractions in college. We already discussed the high level of distraction just your cell phone and other mobile devices present. For many students, getting together and hanging with friends really kicks in as a big diversion from schoolwork. An active social life can become the first priority. And let's be honest, when people reminisce about their grand old college days, I don't imagine that they are thinking of their advanced calculus class. It's the fun and laughable times they remember. Me too! I certainly hope you weave uproarious and memorable social experiences into your college life. But you don't want that at the expense of you academic success.

Here's a suggestion. *Try to think of socializing and partying as your reward for hard work.*

Delay that gratification until you have taken care of your scholarly responsibilities. That is, of course, why you enrolled in college! Remember your social and emotional intelligence and the importance of resisting temptation. That way you create a win-win situation. You successfully complete your assignments AND you have a wonderful time with your friends.

Of course, your personal life, outside of socializing, impacts you and can capture your attention when you are in school as well. While not considered procrastination, things that go on in your life or family including illness, loss, financial problems, the need to work extended hours, and even natural disasters can intrude into your time, focus, and thoughts. They can cause you to put your school work on hold while you address issues involved.

Here it can be helpful to share some of your concerns with your professors. They may be able to afford you extended time to complete your work and make it through the semester.

It can be truly overwhelming to juggle work and school and life. It's a real challenge to get ahead of the curve. While you attend college, it is vital to sit down and realistically structure your time management plan. You might need to let go of some responsibilities and social activities to give yourself adequate time to do quality work.

No worries...I have plenty of time to get this done! Another big reason for procrastination in college is that many assignments are long term. You may have a month or two before an assignment is due. The immediate response is, "Well....I have so much time. No problem." Oh, yes there is a problem! The problem is that the time goes by far more quickly than you would anticipate. Before he knows it, a student is attempting to complete an assignment in just a night or two that was purposely allocated 6-8 weeks to complete because it warranted that amount of time.

With long term projects, many professors will give you the heads up, reminders, and even require progress reports or drafts along the way. This can help keep you on track. However, other professors will not do that. After initially presenting the assignment, they will simply ask for the completed work when the due date comes around. Some students lament and say that they didn't know the project was due. That is why it is very important for students to track assignments; highlight assignments on their syllabus, enter important due dates in their planner, and check on these weekly to make sure they are on top of their assignments.

I didn't know we had to know that!

Realize, too, that your professors may not always cover content in class or assign homework on material that will appear on exams. The expectation is that you read and review material on your own, independently. A professor could indicate that the midterm exam will cover six chapters from your textbook, yet never identify specific pages to read or collect homework on any of the chapters. So once again, it's in your hands.

I just don't want to do it! In fact, I don't think I can!

Sometimes procrastination is really avoidance. A lot of us just don't want to deal with something that is painful, unfamiliar or uncomfortable. If you find that you just can't bring yourself to begin an assignment because you are confused, don't understand the work, or just don't really know how to handle it, remember three things. One is that you are not the only student who feels or who has felt that way. Two is that you need to confront the task rather than let it go. Three is that you should get the help you need in order to move forward.

There are many resources on campus to support you. There are tutorial or help centers throughout the campus and often within each department. Professors regularly hold office hours during which time they are available to meet with students for a variety of reasons, including providing support. But again, it will be up to

you to take charge and to initiate that contact and make
the connection.

**Consider This: What kinds of tasks do you
tend to procrastinate about? Based on what
you read, how might you break up with procrastination, once and for all?**

Meta What? A Few Words about Metacognition

Researchers in psychology view self-monitoring as
part of a larger concept called *metacognition*. In sim-
plest terms, metacognition is thinking about thinking.
It relates to the processes you use to plan, track, and
evaluate your understanding and how you are perform-
ing. It means you have an awareness of your thinking,
your comprehension, and the actions you use to learn.[7]

In a way, metacognition implies that you talk to yourself. You challenge yourself about how you will plan
your day, the tasks you intend to accomplish and how
you will make it happen. It involves asking yourself
many questions to consider before you act.

Let's see how it works with a "To Do" list. Perhaps you
have identified several objectives for the day. These

include: attend three classes, do laundry, exercise, pick up items at the drug store, complete the math and sociology assignments due the next day, and go out for dinner with James.

Metacognition helps you plan and consider the best way for you to accomplish all this. You might say to yourself, "I'm on a tight schedule tomorrow. Since my first class isn't until 10, I'll do a twenty minute yoga workout as soon as I get up. I'll go to classes from 10 to 1:30. Before I leave campus, I'll do my math assignment in the Help Center where it's quiet and I can meet with a tutor on solving the proofs that are still a little confusing to me. It's great that they let me eat there, and that's where I'll have a bite while I'm working. I'll bring my sociology assignment and laptop with me to the laundry room and do the chapter reaction paper right there, rather than going back and forth between cycles. It shouldn't take me more than an hour. (I'll bring my earphones just in case there are people there talking.) That will leave me time to relax a bit before I have dinner with James. He and I can stop at the drug store on the way home and I'll get the toiletries I need."

You also use metacognition to direct your own learning. This occurs before, during, and after you confront a task or assignment. Let's see how....

Before: In anticipation of reading about a topic

or writing a paper, ask yourself, "What do I already know about this topic?" "What do I want to know?" "What do I think I will learn?" "What is the best way for me to handle this assignment?"

During: While you are reading, are in a class, or executing any task on your own, you might ask yourself, "Do I understand what I just read or heard about? Is there something here that is confusing to me?" "Can I pull out what is most important here?" "When should I stop and take a break?" Your responses will guide you to either move forward, take another look, or identify in your mind (and perhaps in your notes) the most important points.

After: Following your involvement in a learning process, you might ask yourself, "Do I understand the material I worked on?" "What was the most significant point here? How does what I learned differ from what I thought before this process?" "What new questions do I now have?" "Did I spend my time wisely?" "Did I cover all the material I wanted to get through?"

Using metacognition, you also actively consider your process. "What was the best method for me to plan and organize my paper?" "What strategies did I use that helped me understand the chapter in my textbook?"

"What's the best way for me to review my material?"
"How do I know when I have studied enough?"

Thinking about your thinking and about how you learn best helps you monitor your own process and progress. If forces you to identify methods and strategies that work best for you, and to consider alternatives until you find them.

———⋙◉⋘———

Getting good at self-monitoring is very empowering. The better you do, the more confident you will feel in your own capacity to run and manage your life... and all you set out to accomplish....successfully. This will be in school and beyond. It does wonders for your self-esteem!

Consider This: Think about a long term assignment you have in one of your classes, or about the tasks in a day you would like to complete. Use metacognition to organize and/or direct the process involved in completing it successfully. List the specific steps you need, and how you will accomplish them, to complete your objective.

CHAPTER 9

Feel for Others:
Being Empathic

> "....when we focus on others, our world expands. Our own problems drift to the periphery of the mind and so seem smaller, and we increase our capacity for connection - or compassionate action."

— *Daniel Goleman, psychologist and author, from Social Intelligence: The New Science of Human Relationships*

> "No one cares how much you know, until they know how much you care."

— *Theodore Roosevelt, 26th U.S. President*

This chapter is all about something called empathy. Be sure not to confuse it with *sympathy*. Sympathy is feeling sorrow or pity for the misfortune of another person. Empathy is different. For now, here's a quick definition. It's the capacity to see and experience the world as another person would. You may wonder what it is doing in a book about triumphing in school, but you will soon understand how being empathic supports you throughout a wide range of college experiences.

Let me begin with a scenario in which I expressed empathy to one of my students. Even though it couldn't change the outcome of a particular situation, it helped create a connection that became very valuable at a later time.

Kiara's Story

Kiara was a freshman in my Reading 101 class a few years ago. She came to see me during my office hour at the start of the fourth week of the fall semester. Our class had met seven times by then, but Kiara had made it to only three of the classes. So she was already beyond the "limit" of absences that were permitted to receive a grade for that class.

Also, Kiara had not completed any of the readings or assignments for class. This was because she still hadn't obtained her textbook. For students who had financial issues that made it tough to purchase the book, I had recommended that they use the copy that was on reserve in the library. They could also borrow the book from me or a fellow student, or make copies of some of the assigned pages from a desk copy in the department office. Access to the book was important, not only to enrich understanding of the class discussions, but to complete several of the assignments. Unfortunately, Kiara had not chosen to take any of the options. So she was terribly behind in her work.

She had come to my office to let me know that she would be missing three more classes in the coming weeks before the midterm. She explained that she had many personal family issues that needed her attention. She might not even make it to the midterm, but said she would try to make it up. She wanted to remain in the class.

To get the whole picture, you should be aware of the good news as well. On those three days when Kiara had attended class she was a superstar! She asked a lot of questions, offered up thoughtful comments to our discussions, and showed a lot of interest and potential. She worked well with her fellow students in small groups and even showed leadership qualities. I tell you this, so you can understand how difficult it was for me to say what I needed to say to her....

I felt deeply for Kiara's personal dilemmas, but didn't see any way for her to realistically continue in the class. She had "no idea" about the material we had been discussing. She was far behind in her work submission. She hadn't handed in any assignments! And, as you know, her attendance was totally below the standards set for class. She would not be present for the midterm exam. She was even too far behind to take a grade of "Incomplete" in the course, which is sometimes offered to students who finish the class, but haven't submitted some of the required coursework before the close of the semester. They are given a period of time, following the conclusion of the semester, to turn in missing work and earn a grade.

Kiara would be welcome to continue attending class when she could, but that would not be good enough to be awarded a grade for the course. We talked for over an hour. I conveyed to her my understanding of her problems, as well as my concern. I understood her disappointment and frustration. I shared a story with her about a time in my own life when I had to step away from a project I had begun because I just couldn't give it the time it warranted. I wanted Kiara to know that I realized how difficult this time was for her. I knew how hard it was to give up something one had started, with so much hope and motivation. After our meeting I learned that Kiara had withdrawn from all of her courses and taken a leave of absence from the college.

Fast forward two semesters later. I spotted Kiara's name on my class roster. Wow...she was back! I was thrilled. I reached out to her before she left the classroom that first day. I wanted to extend a personal welcome back. Kiara shared that, yes, she had been really "bummed out" having to withdraw from class the year before. But at the same time, she left feeling unburdened by sharing her problems and was deeply appreciative of my willingness to listen, be there for her, and communicate understanding. She hadn't left feeling angry or totally blown away. She left feeling understood. She knew, deep down in her motivated self, that one day she would be back. Actually, stepping away was a good choice. Leaving the class helped free her to take care of what she needed to do at home and rid her of the stress she was constantly under about missing class!

Kiara was present and focused upon her return and was able to work to her potential. Yup, she got an A in the class. However, the point of this story isn't only about Kiara's success. It's about the impact of empathy. When you experience it from another, as Kiara did from me, you know it and it feels great. It may not change the situation, but somehow makes it more tolerable. It's like taking a deep breath and feeling a little less alone. When you can exude it to others, are empathic to those around you, you are giving a gift to them as well. I have come to believe that Kiara was able to leave and to come back to college, because when she left, she knew she had a safe place to which she could return.

The Power of Empathy

Empathy is the ability to sense or feel the world as another person; even when those feelings or concerns are unspoken. It is the capacity to share, understand and ultimately to respond to another person's feelings, needs, concerns and/or emotional state.[1, 2] Being empathic is a cornerstone of social and emotional intelligence.

Though empathy is experienced personally, inside of you, it greatly impacts your response to your outside world. It affects how you communicate and relate to all those with whom you connect and interact. This includes those who you may meet with casually, like your classmate, professor, coach, or even the librarian at school. Of course it affects your interaction with more personally significant connections in your life, like your partner, parents, or bff.

Empathy enables us to put aside our own perceptions and focus, and take the perspective of another. Daniel Goleman calls it our social radar. Empathy leads us to caring, compassion, and altruism, which is the showing of concern for others. In a world challenged by "isms," i.e. nationalism, racism, lookism, sexism, having empathy helps break down biases and engenders tolerance and the acceptance of differences.[3]

That is an amazing capacity.

Empathic people tend to reach out and help others. They are adept at understanding, so are less likely to misread or misjudge and find themselves in conflict. People with empathy are more likely to develop social expertise.[4] In a broad sense, empathy moves us from a self-centered, egotistical state, where we focus on ourselves, to a more people-centered, humanistic mindset. Here, we truly consider others. The focus is on how we respond to or support them with compassion.

Let's consider several ways empathy can help you in college. Above all, empathy enables you to forge connections and relationships. (We will consider just how important this is in the following chapter on socialization.) As is the case with all of the components of social and emotional intelligence, empathy can grow and develops stronger, especially once you become conscious of it.

The Benefits of Empathy

· **Empathy Enhances Perspective Taking**

Abraham Lincoln once said "When I get ready to talk to people, I spend two thirds of the time thinking what they want to hear and one third thinking about what I want to say."

Putting yourself in the place of another person and imagining how you would feel as that person is the essence of empathy. Taking the perspective of others can filter into your interactions with most everyone, including professors, friends, family members and the cashier at the check-out counter!

Empathy raises your sensitivity to the people you study or learn about, from the past or in our modern world. Having the capacity to see and feel through the eyes of someone else deepens your level of understanding, and compassion, and moves you to behave in an accepting and even kinder way of being. How did soldiers feel landing on the shores of Normandy? What could a person be thinking or feeling when they are refused admission to a club because of their race or gender identification? How does it feel to be bullied? To be transsexual? Falsely accused? Falsely convicted? Taken into slavery? Lose an election? Be abandoned or abused? To declare war? To surrender? To rescue animals?

As you study people and societies from the past, from other cultures or parts of the world, or from various socioeconomic and educational levels, having an empathic frame of reference will strengthen your learning. You will be better able to understand their motives, thinking, and actions; bringing sensitivity and a capacity to relate.

Empathy can help you adjust or monitor your own behavior in class. Seeing things from the perspective of your professor can influence the way you choose to respond or interact in class. It helps you know when it's time to stay quiet or attentive, interject a question or not, decide if it's ok to fool around, bring in a sandwich, crack a joke, talk with others, or even leave the class early for one reason or another. Your sense of "where your professor is at" with these things comes with your capacity to take his or her point of view, be respectful of it, and adjust your own behavior as a result of your sensitivities. You may ultimately decide to come to class on time not just because you don't want to be marked "late," but because you understand how devalued your professor may feel when students saunter in fifteen minutes after class has begun. Or you may choose to never text in class, because you too find it rude and discounting when someone does that to you in the middle of a personal conversation. You know how it feels.

As you meet and interact with a wider group of fellow students than ever before, who come from different areas, backgrounds, cultures, races and walks of life, your empathy will enable you to accept differences and find common ground. You will be more likely to abandon judgements and connect with a more open mind and open heart.

- **Empathy Helps you Recognize Emotion in Others**

Have you ever met anyone you thought of as "clueless?" Actually, we tend to use this rather pejorative term to describe a person who just "doesn't get it" though all the signs of a particular message are there. The message is not stated directly, or even expressed in words, but it is clearly sent - just not received. This can occur in relationships. It's often a close friend who has to say, "Don't you get it. He's (or She's) just not into you!"

Reading the emotions of others is an offshoot of empathy. Empathic people recognize emotions in others, even if the emotion is not stated. Perhaps this is because they can draw upon their own range of feelings in any given situation. They are adept at noticing and interpreting non-verbal cues including gestures, eye-contact, facial expressions, and body language.

Besides the actual content of a verbal exchange, emotions are revealed through the pace of the speech, choice of particular words, and the tone and volume of voice. People with empathy are alert to these nuances and variations. They spot the "clues" to the real meaning and emotions behind a conversation. You may know that the inability to read is sometimes called dyslexia. Interestingly, the inability to "read" emotions in others is sometimes referred to as social dyslexia.

Being astute at recognizing emotions in others is critical to effective communication and relationship building. In college, you want to be attuned to the feelings of those around you. This helps you make better choices during your exchanges; whether to move forward or back, continue to speak or stop to listen, choose to use formal language rather than slang, or even decide to leave someone's room rather than stay. You want to sense you might be pressing someone's emotional buttons by continuing to pursue a topic that they no longer wish to discuss, or know when someone would welcome your support.

Students who can express their needs in a style that engenders respect, understanding, and compassion in others are at a real advantage. Think of the how well this can serve you when asking for support or consideration from a friend or a professor. What a disadvantage the "clueless" person is at by being demanding, confrontational, or threatening.

- **Empathic People are Good Listeners**

"I know you hear me, but are you really listening?"

Do you see the distinction here? If you do, then you

know there is a difference between hearing something, a function of auditory acuity, and truly listening, a more cognitive, and social/emotional skill. Most of us have never been taught how to listen, let alone to listen empathetically.

Empathic listening goes beyond listening to learn information or content, as you might in a lecture or presentation. It involves listening to understand feelings or a point of view. Its goal is to improve mutual understanding and trust.

Empathic listening, also called active or reflective listening, is often used in negotiations to resolve disputes or conflicts. It is just as an important tool to consider in our everyday lives and relationships. We would do well to listen to those who matter to us with the idea that we want to understand their point of view, or problem, and how they feel. This kind of listening builds trust and respect, and creates a safe environment that leads to collaboration and problem solving. [5]

Even if we can't change a situation, others truly appreciate being understood, without judgement or criticism. This kind of communication forges friendships and relationships. We need it to work well with others; be they our companions and friends in life, our partners in chemistry lab, members of our small group in psychology class, or teammates on the football field.

So how do you listen with empathy? In its truest sense, as you listen you convey your understanding, without criticism or judgment. You provide a sounding board and an understanding ear.

When you listen empathically, it is not about waiting your turn to make your own point or to solve the problem. Mostly, you will verbalize your non-judgmental responses. You might say, "Yes, I understand." Or "I see, tell me more." If you are speaking to a friend, you might reflect back what they are saying to you. For example, when you bump into your friend who is very upset about a C- he received on his most recent essay, you might say something like, "I see. You really feel your paper deserved a higher grade and are really frustrated because you spent so many hours working on it. I know how you must feel."

Of course, as a friend you may feel compelled to get more involved. You might provide help, offer advice, or try to do something to draw your friend out of his unhappiness. However, keep in mind that very often just your listening, hearing, and understanding can be invaluable to your buddy. It is a meaningful gift that provides relief and sensitivity on their road to coping or problem solving.

Being a good listener also implies that you set aside your own needs for a while, and really allow others to vent and express their views. Forget about being patient just to have *your* chance to speak, come up with *your* advice, or tell *your* opinion. Give up your own ideas for a while and truly listen. This not only fosters relationship, understanding and problem solving, but is an important capacity for developing leadership.

You might find yourself taking steps in this direction while you are in college. Perhaps you will lead a small group of fellow students in a collaborative activity in one of your classes, become the president of a club you join, or become an officer in the student government on campus. Being a good listener will definitely help you evolve into a better leader.

- **Empathy Forges Connection**

Above all else, empathy fosters your ability to relate to and connect with those on your campus and in your life. Your ability to take the perspective of others, your sensitivity to the people around you, and the compassion you feel and emote, creates the foundation of your personal environment. Use your empathy to reach out to the people who inhabit the world of college with you. From your roommates and classmates, to the dorm monitors, sorority sisters, fraternity brothers, professors, counselors, public safety officers, administrative personnel or cafeteria workers, the commonality you find will welcome you and help you feel that you belong.

Also, remember that when you want to be there for a troubled friend, you don't always need to have a solution to their problems. Writer Maya Angelou commented that we recall how we felt in the company of people, often more so than what we may have done or discussed. Empathy is all about helping people feel heard, understood, and accepted.

Consider This: Think of a time someone showed you empathy. How did it make you feel? Have you ever thought a teacher or professor was empathic to you? How did that work out? What kind of empathy do you anticipate your professors would want from you, as their student?

CHAPTER 10

You're Not Alone: Forging Social Skills and Making Connections in College

"The glory of friendship is not the outstretched hand, not the kindly smile, nor the joy of companionship; it is the spiritual inspiration that comes to one when you discover that someone else believes in you and is willing to trust you with a friendship."

— *Ralph Waldo Emerson, American essayist and poet*

When it comes to forming affiliations and connections, going to college is like entering a new universe…and then merging into a matrix of several smaller ones.

Immediately you identify as a member of a future graduating class, ie. The class of 2024, 2025 and so on. You join others as a freshman, sophomore, junior, or senior. Your name appears on a class roster, and thus you become a member of the group of students in the course you take, whether in a classroom, lab, studio, on the athletic field, or online. You may have one or two roommates in a dorm room, or several in a suite or apartment. Perhaps you become part of a bunch of friends who regularly lunch together at the student union or hang out at a club or a restaurant. You might expand your affiliations even more by participating in a campus-wide club, study group, service organization, athletic team, sorority, or fraternity. At its best, college is a social world as well as an academic one.

Whether at work or play, your ability to relate well with others in college is important for a satisfying personal experience and, as we will discuss, for your academic success. For sure, your interpersonal connections with others can help you really enjoy your college days and triumph.

All of the SEI components we have discussed, self-awareness, the regulation and management of your emotions, motivation and goal setting, keeping track of your efforts and self-monitoring, and especially empathy, play major roles in your ability to forge friendships and sustain positive personal connections in college. Social skills, in and of themselves, are a component of your social and emotional intelligence.

Get Connected

Connections at college can have both immediate and long lasting impact. Actually, I met my lifetime BFF on my first day as an undergraduate. Cathy was one of two roommates in my freshman dorm room. No one could make me laugh like she did, and still does. Frankly, no one else has ever come close. On a deeper level, we tended to share our feelings openly and always learned from one another. Though we both became educators, our lives placed us on divergent paths and we haven't always lived close to one another. But we are still best friends today, almost half a century later.

Actually, when you reminisce with someone who attended college, there's a good chance they'll recall social escapades, relationships, and fun times with friends, far more readily than the papers they wrote or the topics they studied! *Ah yes, college was great. I remember the time we all went skinny dipping in Lake Cayuga. It was 40 degrees and we laughed our heads off. Then Brian stole everyone's clothes, so we.....yada...yada...yada.*

But beyond the fun and laughs, you may be surprised to realize that good interpersonal skills find their way into your studies as well. Yes, you might have class in a large lecture hall, being one of hundreds of students listening to a presentation and with next to no exchange of ideas among your classmates. But, hopefully, you will also be part of smaller, more collaborative learning experiences. Many instructors intentionally design their lessons to be interactive and dynamic, so that students work together and get to know one another. This is a time to participate, ask and answer questions, and engage in a juicy class discussion!

Collaborative learning is a great way to enjoy the coursework, generate ideas, and build skills for your future in the world of work. You might pair up with a classmate on an assignment, problem solve in a small group in class, or be part of an ongoing classroom team. Outside of class you might partner with other students to research or study together. Forming study groups can really offset the isolation that is sometimes generated from a large, impersonal, lecture hall class situation. It is a supportive pathway to connect with fellow students.

Connect with your professors, too. Typically, they care deeply about their teaching and their students. Most often, they are approachable, concerned about your welfare, and eager to help in any way they can. Some of your teachers may become important mentors, advisors, or even confidants in your life. You will want to forge positive relationships with them all, using good social judgment and effective communication skills. Reach out to them, both in and outside of class.

Let's consider the social skills that will enrich your time in school. While we will address these through the view screen of a college student, it's not a big stretch to see how they will play a part throughout your adult life, in your personal relationships and even in the workplace.

The Top 6 Social Skills to Triumph in College

1. Be Open to New Relationships

"You can make more friends in two months by becoming really interested in other people than you can in two years by trying to get other people interested in you. Which is just another way of saying that the way to make a friend is to be one." [1]

— Dale Carnegie, American writer on personal
development and public speaking

One of the scariest things about attending college is that you're heading to a place where you likely don't know anyone….and they don't know you! That's a bit daunting, yet everyone is in the same boat.

On the flip side, it's really quite awesome. You have a golden opportunity to wipe the slate clean and begin anew. Going to college is a time that you can "start over," reboot, or even reinvent yourself. You can approach others based on who you are now, rather than who you have been, or been judged to be. What a breath of fresh air.

Even if you head to a local university or community college rather than go 'away' to school, you are likely to meet people from many different walks of life. Your campus neighborhood will probably be far more diverse than you have previously experienced. It likely will include students and faculty of various religions, cultures, traditions, races, sexual orientations, gender identifications, political views and socio-economic backgrounds. Getting to know them; their views, experiences, and stories is another way you become a more worldly person in college. As you experience and connect with a wider group of peers, you are likely to become a more accepting and tolerant individual. And despite this range of differences, you have at least one thing in common with every single other student on campus. You attend the same school! Yes, commonality!

2. Join In

Sometimes joining in and making connections feels difficult, if not challenging. This is especially true on a commuter campus, where you travel to school daily and then leave. Everyone is coming and going, often quickly departing campus as soon as classes are over. Students rush off to deal with the other parts of their lives, like going to work, tending to family responsibilities, or just taking time to relax.

But keep this is mind. Student satisfaction surveys tell us that the more ways in which you can engage with others and activities at school, the happier you will be. You are also more likely to persist in the pursuit of your goals and even graduate. So try not to run right back to your dorm or drive off campus as soon as classes are over. Hang around for a while! Join in.

Enrich your college life with activities you enjoy and do them with others. Go out for the team. Join a club and meet fellow students who like to cook, act, exercise, build, write, sing, help, paint, dance, or whatever the focus of the club might be. Some clubs are organized to bring like-minded people together; those who have the same religion, ethnic or cultural heritage, and or sexual orientation. You might welcome this connection, in addition to reaching out to something new.

As you look for commonality, try to embrace differences as well. Be open to forging new friendships and relationships. Even if this means stepping out of your comfort zone, try to reach out to another person or several other students in each of your classes with whom you might typically not have connected.

Having a "go to" person in every class is great if you ever have a question about the course material or are absent and want to find out what you've missed. Sometimes it's just a matter of having the nerve to ask for someone's cell phone number. Perhaps one will become a study partner. Aside from the practical benefits, it is just nice to have a friend or two in class. Have confidence in your capacity to take that first step. The more you do it, the more natural reaching out will become. Though you might consider yourself a private person, the quality of your college experience will surely be enhanced if it includes connections with others.

3. Communicate Effectively...With Self-Awareness and Empathy

"We are more advanced technologically than ever before. However, technology, in many respects, is leading to the decline of conversation." [2]

— *Cindy Ann Peterson, author and public speaker*

Thousands of books have been written about effective communication. We all want to be understood and have our words convey what we mean, need, think, or feel. It's so frustrating to be misunderstood. Conversely, we want to comprehend what other people are conveying to us, both on an informational level and an emotional one. We don't want to "not get it" or misunderstand.

Technology offers us many venues to express ourselves. Emails, texts, posts and tweets get our messages out there, quickly and concisely. But ironically, because electronic language is so often scaled down, sometimes real intentions, and lots of emotions, get "lost in translation." Messaging doesn't always convey the feelings and tones that inhabit spoken language. Nor does it include the visual cues we send out with our facial expressions.

Writer Cindy Peterson states that we may be losing our ability to just have a conversation! Talking with others is an important vehicle for establishing connection. You want to get along with the new people you meet; make friends and have meaningful relationships. To do that, it is still is important to be able to strike up a conversation and have it go well.

As a professor, some of my most memorable moments with students have occurred when someone stops into my office for one reason or another, because this usually leads to a chat. The encounter might start off as a mid-year conference, a meeting to discuss an assignment, or even a session to make up an exam. But when that's finished, a conversion often begins. Inevitably, this becomes a time for me to see and appreciate the person who is my student. It's like a veil is lifted!

Through these informal office chats I've learned a lot about students. I learned of Tamika's unique aspirations to earn a certificate in mortuary science so she can run her family's funeral home. (She is the only person I've ever known who has actually taken part in embalming!) I really came to understand how difficult commuting to and from school can be after Sean explained about the two crosstown busses he takes, in snowstorms and rain, to get to campus. I was able to put Samuel in touch with a counselor after he told me about his problems with substance abuse. (He's much better now.) And I must admit, I love it when a student reveals that something I said in class meant a lot to them personally or "opened their eyes" to see something in a new or different way. Conversations generate connection. So don't back away from opportunities to engage, especially with peers and your professors.

So for sure, in college you will come in contact with people of different backgrounds, cultures and perspectives. You will want to listen well, and hopefully, be accepting of differences and alternative points of view. Ask questions to learn more. Try to be less inclined to argue, judge or certainly denigrate the opinions of others. Listen attentively and try to understand.

4. Express Yourself

Conversely, you want to be comfortable articulating your own views, needs, opinions and values. You will want to advocate for yourself. To do this effectively, you will call upon many of the SEI elements we've discussed.

Whether it's telling the captain of your soccer team the position you'd like to play, the campus security guard

why you shouldn't get a parking violation, or your professor where you want to sit in class, you will access
your social and emotional intelligence to advocate for
yourself productively. Your self-awareness; knowledge
of your own needs and preferences, your empathy; a
sense of how the receiver of your information feels and
your insight about how to communicate to engender
the response you desire, and your capacity to regulate
your emotions so you are rational and calm, will help
you express yourself articulately.

Strive to communicate in a way that generates respect
and understanding. This can be a real game changer
with your professors. For example, say you feel you deserve a higher grade on your research paper. You did
everything you were supposed to do. You answered all
the questions posed by the assignment, located and
used several good sources to back up your point of
view, submitted the required five pages, and put a lot
of time and effort into your work. Man, the C+ you received just doesn't seem fair. You want to advocate for
a higher grade on your paper. How will you do it?

Your empathic side needs to consider what a professor
wants. Well, I can tell you that he or she wants students to express their views, but with respect, clarity,
and courtesy. You will need to regulate any anger you
feel regarding the grade you received, and your sense
of unfairness on the part of the professor. It would be

fine to remind the professor of all you attempted to do accurately, but be willing to hear what you might have done "better." Learn from the experience. Rather than argue, perhaps you could ask how you might revise your paper for a stronger grade.

Try using "I" messages, rather than "You" messages when expressing your feelings. Speaking with your professor, it would be better to say, "I was disappointed with the grade I received on this paper," or ask "Where did I misstep?" and "What can I do to improve it?" rather than, "Why did you fail me?" or "You didn't explain what we had to do." When you "own" your statements, rather than approach others with an accusatory or blameful "You," you set a tone for a reasonable and non-confrontational dialogue. It is more likely to lead to the outcome you desire.

By the way, "I" messages are also helpful when you want to clarify or communicate your understanding of what someone else has said. You reiterate what you "heard." For example, to make sure you understand an assignment, after class you might approach your professor by saying, "So as I understand it, we are to read the first three chapters and then outline the main points in each section. Is that correct?" Or you tell your friend, "Then It sounds to me like you want to set a new meeting schedule for next week because you would like more time to work on Part 2. Right?" In this way you can make sure you have understood what has been said, and do not bring an immediate judgement or reaction to the exchange.

5. Work Collaboratively in Groups

Socially and emotionally intelligent people know how to work well with others. This is true in life, as it is in college. In fact, the experiences you have in college that challenge you to work cooperatively with your fellow students will help prepare you for such tasks as you move out into the workplace and become part of a larger community.

In school you are likely to find yourself part of a pair, group, or team...charged with a specific task or objective. There are many ways this could happen. You may be assigned a partner in a science lab, be part of small groups in sociology class that each address a different topical question, be selected as a team member in an athletic class, or work as part of the editorial staff for the college newspaper. In all these situations, collaboration will be vital to take on and complete the task. Community service or service learning experiences, now often a part of academic life, call upon your skills to work cooperatively with others.

What does cooperative collaboration involve? Actually, it incorporates all of the social skills we have discussed.

Certainly, it means actively listening to others. You will also have to be flexible and consider multiple alternatives or plans to tackle a task. As a collaborator or team member, it's only right to contribute your fair share and not leave all the work to others. A good collaborator expresses his or her views without putting others down. And, like you learned in kindergarten, you need to take turns rather than take over. Cooperative collaboration holds the keys to enriched and satisfying group experiences.

And should problems arise, tip number 6 should really help.

6. Resolve Conflicts in a Productive and Caring Way

We all know that no matter how hard we may try, conflicts do occur. People just see things differently and have opposing points of view. Sometimes one decision needs to win out.

Solving disputes is not easy. If everyone had the skills to work through conflicts smoothly, we wouldn't need lawyers, arbitrators, judges, negotiators, mediators, psychologists, and counselors. (All interesting professions, by the way.) Getting passed differences can get pretty intense, and takes certain skills. There's even a master's degree for conflict resolution.

Of course, you don't want to hire the services of a professional to help you work through arguments or differing opinions with your roommate or friends. You want to be able to resolve disagreements on your own, with the least amount of trauma and hard feelings.

Being able to harmonize diverse feelings is an important skill for you to nurture as you move through your adult life. At college, the more adept you are at being able to do this, the more peaceful and happy you will feel.

Sometimes differences of opinion can be stimulating, exciting, and motivating. They make for the best debates, lively class discussions, and motivate the creation of action plans to change the world. But when they exist on a personal level, conflict and confrontation can create a lot of stress and dysphoria. You have a lot on your plate at school, and you don't want disagreements or arguments to get the better of you or crowd your emotional self.

Several of the suggestions for working collaboratively can help you avoid conflicts in the first place. First and foremost, try to get a handle on your own emotions and manage them so that your exchanges are productive and helpful, rather than combative or antagonistic. Try to remain sensitive to the mindset of others and be open to alternative perspectives. Be flexible and allow for some wiggle room, even when you just can't wait to get your point across. Consider where and how you might adjust your own thinking. Be open to changing your mind. Choose your words carefully at times, and try to communicate in a way that is friendly, kind, or even humorous, but not hostile, demeaning, defensive, or accusatory.

Ironically, sometimes dealing with confrontations and getting to the other side of the disagreement brings people closer together. Try to use disputes as opportunities to really hear another person and, who knows, perhaps you will go on to establish an even greater connection.

Resolving Conflicts: Tips to Make It Better

Here are several tips for dealing with and resolving conflicts in school. I think they will help you through some tough spots.

- **Try to stay calm.** You need to get a handle on your emotions before you attempt to engage. You want to think clearly and rationally. For example, if you are planning to speak with your professor about a grade that offends you, don't go storming into her office! Cool off. Make an appointment. Think about what you want to say. Even jot down key points. It's ok to show your concern, but you still want to present yourself in a good light; rational, thoughtful, and caring.

- **Listen both to what people are saying and what they are feeling.** You need to understand another point of view in order to respond to it intelligently and compassionately. Interestingly, your capacity to let another person know that you "get it," strengthens the validity of your own response. Use your empathic listening skills, ie. "I think you are saying that...." Or "I'm hearing that you are upset about ...". If you are able to convey your understanding, the person with whom you are at odds is likely to be pleased and more inclined to continue discussion in a positive light. Be aware of how deeply others feel about the words they are expressing and use that insight to help you adjust how far you go or how long you continue your exchange.

- **Stay in the moment.** Especially if you have a charged history with someone, try to focus on the issue at hand, rather than holding on to past differences. If you rehash old wounds, it will be harder to resolve a current issue and move on.

- **Don't take it personally.** As leaders in the business world often say, most disagreements aren't personal in nature. They result from truly different viewpoints or approaches. Rather than arguing a choice or solution, spend more time focusing on the underlying reasons that drive your choice or conclusion. [3] Don't feel that it is about you or the person with whom you are disputing. Stay focused on the issue and the outcome.

- **You don't always need to win.** Sometimes knowing when to back down, even if you think you are in the right, is a wise thing to do. This is especially true when you are interested in harmony and maintaining a relationship. [4] It's helpful to be empathic here, and try to understand how the other side can, indeed, have a point. Realize that you are not losing, but making a choice. Your friend may, in fact, always end up picking the movie you see. However, if they are selecting a show that you really don't mind seeing as well, let go of the power struggle and enjoy!

- **Choose your battles.** It takes a lot of energy to go to war! Consider the importance of what you may be "fighting" for. Not everything is worth your effort. [5] You have a lot to contend with in the course of your college week, so if your roommate didn't make their bed one day, or didn't return your book when they said they would, well, let it go...especially if they bring it back the next day. If someone keeps you waiting, use the time to read or check messages, rather than fume because they are late. Try to be as peaceful as you can be, whenever you can. There are a lot of legitimate stresses at school, so "don't sweat the small stuff."

- **Be willing to acknowledge your part.** Sometimes the truth in a dispute is somewhere in the middle of both sides. The best resolutions are based on compromise. Each party doesn't lose everything and everyone wins a little bit. Be strong enough to be flexible, honest enough to admit your own role in a problematic situation, and wise enough to give in, albeit a little, for the sake of moving on. And if it's appropriate, saying, "I'm sorry" can go a long way to assuage negative feelings and hurt.

- **Don't be afraid to ask for help.** Be smart enough to ask for assistance in dealing with a dispute when you need it. You might benefit from a sounding board to let off steam, or from the advice, of a friend, professor, or counselor. There may be times when a third, impartial party can be of help by intervening, hearing both sides, and offering solution options. Living in a dorm, if there is a problem you might go to the RA to seek his or her counsel. If you find yourself at odds with any college personnel, including a professor, you might wish to speak with a department chairperson or dean, to get advice or actually intervene to help mediate the problem.

- **Try to forgive.** Ironically, the capacity to forgive may do more emotionally for the person who has been wronged, i.e., the "victim," than for the "perpetrator" of the "crime." Forgiveness frees the person who has been harmed from being controlled by their hurt. Hold on to this idea. When you stay in the throes of anger and hurt, with a desire to punish or take revenge, it drains your energy, colors your mood, and zaps your ability to be happy. You need your energy and focus in college, and certainly deserve happiness. So, to the extent that you can forgive and release negative thoughts, the better you will feel. When possible, move on. Let go of the negativity. Be happy. Mahatma Gandhi, the inspirational civil rights leader of India, told us that forgiveness takes strength. Be strong.

Consider this: Which of the strategies above to you tend to use to help you through conflicts? Going forward, which might you consider trying out?

Step Up to Leadership

College is a great place to step out, take a chance, and try something new. Even if you have never before taken on a leadership position, seize the opportunities in college. Try to take charge in some way, big or small. You don't always need to be elected or even appointed as a "leader." Don't hesitate to volunteer for the role... and see how it feels.

You learn a lot in college, and not only in academics. Your willingness to experience new roles, including that of leader, will resonate with you long after you leave school, and help prepare you for future roles you may take on in your family, the workplace, and in your community. Who knows? You may come away with a new definition of yourself and career path just as a result of trying out a leadership role.

Leaders are about the good of the whole. When you think about what really makes a good leader, perhaps you will agree that they are about integrity and trust. Leaders are motivated and motivating. Rather than being just "the boss", real leadership is about listening, planning, team building and relating.

As you move forward in leadership experiences you will really call upon your social and emotional intelligence. You will want to be self-aware and exude trust and confidence, be in control of your emotions, have ideas for the future, be able to set goals, call upon your self-monitoring and organizational skills, show empathy and sensitivity to the needs and feelings of others, get along well and work cooperatively. Embracing the social and emotional qualities we have discussed will help guide and prepare you for leadership.

If leadership is new to you, start small. People often shy away from being in charge (It can be a little scary and uh-oh, maybe it's too much work!) so just by default, as others back away, you may come across several opportunities to step up to the plate. If you join a club, be willing to become an officer of some sort... the president, vice-resident, secretary, or treasurer. If you're feeling hesitant, perhaps you can begin by sharing a position, such as a co-chair, or co-president. Or consider a stint as a vice-president, before moving on to the top position.

In your classes, if small groups are formed to carry out tasks and roles of leadership are called for, volunteer to be the leader, or director. You may be surprised by how you do, and how you feel simply by taking on a bit of responsibility to get things done. You will learn skills along the way.

Student government on college campuses offers many opportunities to get involved and draws you into many new and interesting encounters. At the college where I teach, members of student government sit in on the Academic Senate of Faculty and Administrators, and truly have a voice in the policy making of that body.

You may have an idea that you want to make happen or a cause or charity that you want to support. There are many opportunities to take initiative on campus. If you have an idea about something, and also ideas about how to make it happen, then go for it. Talk with your friends or professors, advisors, or counselors, to learn of pathways that may be available to you to take on a leadership role.

Being a leader doesn't necessarily mean taking on a titled position. In any situation where you have an opportunity to assert your views or opinions, well then, go for it. Express yourself! Do this in class, in activities, and hanging with your friends. Consider how you can influence others to go along with your ideas, plans, or views for the commonn good. Being confident and persuasive are important qualities for any leader. Be so in a way that engenders cooperation and collaboration.

And in Conclusion...Be nice!
· ·

In 1986, author Robert Fulghum wrote a bestselling book called *All I Really Need to Know I Learned in Kindergarten.*[6] The messages he invokes are simple.

Ironically, for you at the other end of the educational spectrum in college, they really do apply. Some of my favorites are to play fair, say you're sorry when you've hurt someone, share, be kind to one another, clean up after your mess, and hold hands and stick together. Remember these?

The point is that as you negotiate your social life and times in school, and the world, you will come more and more in touch with the virtues of caring, kindness, and just being a nice person. Perhaps you are already there....perhaps you'd like to try harder. In any case, being mindful of others, giving of yourself, showing respect, and even some manners, are qualities that will make your life, and the lives of those around you, a little bit sweeter.

Consider This: What are some ways you have been a leader in your life so far? What might hold you back, when a part of you wants to step up? In what ways might you take on a leadership role in college?

CHAPTER 11

Be Your Best Self: Putting Your Powers to Work

Heading to college with an understanding of social and emotional intelligence, and applying it to your day to day challenges and experiences, will truly help you triumph. It's as though you have the tools to be your own life coach!

I believe SEI forges the foundation of your learning, your pleasure in scholarly pursuits, your capacity to make and sustain relationships, and your ultimate collegiate success. Reread pages and call upon strategies to help you manage yourself, your time, and your studies, and to persist even through difficulties and challenges.

A magnificent quality of SEI is that it continues to grow throughout your life. Your intention to consider and strengthen the capacities that create your social and emotional self will help you flourish during your college years...and serve you far beyond those times into the rest of your life.

- **Self-awareness** will enable you to make the best choices for yourself; select your friends, decide what to do to make yourself happy and comfortable, and know what activities or people to avoid. It will help your academic choices regarding what and how many courses to take, when to take them, and how much and how best to study. You will understand the reasons and circumstances for your emotions rather than be blown away by them. You will be able to discuss and describe your feelings and be your own best advocate. With self-awareness you will know yourself and be true to yourself.

- **Regulating your emotions** will help you to respond reasonably and thoughtfully to the ups and downs of your college experience. The capacity to regulate your emotions will enable you to manage your moods, hurts, and frustrations and tolerate difficulties or disappointment. You will have strategies to cope with stressors and to self-soothe, rather than act out in self-destructive ways. You will manage your feelings in productive and positive ways that serve your best interests. Perhaps your optimism will grow as well.

- **Setting you goals**; short term, intermediate, and long term, will help keep you motivated. Evaluating and adjusting your goals throughout your college years will keep them in your consciousness and carve out meaningful and doable pathways to achieve them. Your eye on the prize will serve you well to work hard and attain it.

- **Self-monitoring** will enable you to be a good friend to yourself. You will be the captain of your own ship, decide how you are doing, and make changes along the way so your journey is successful and satisfying. Self-monitoring will enable you to manage your time - a real challenge for college students - and delay gratification so that you stay on target, persist, and persevere in the face of difficulties or distractions. Access your grit and persist to meet the goals you have set for yourself.

- **Empathy** will pervade your thinking and your behavior. Perceiving and understanding others will serve you well. Putting yourself in their place, imagining how you would feel as that person, will enrich your relatedness to those you encounter in college. Of course, these include your friends, classmates and professors. But your scholarly world will go further and so can your empathy. It will encompass characters in the literature you read, people in cultures you consider in anthropology or sociology, leaders and revolutionaries throughout history you will study, researchers in the sciences and technologies you explore, and performers and creators in the arts in which you engage and enjoy. Being empathic will heighten your sensitivity to others. It will help you listen effectively, resolve conflict, create harmony, and present yourself as a person of compassion and understanding.

- *Social skills* will allow you to happily participate in the world with others. Your capacity to engage with friends and professors, to collaborate, to inspire, to work with and to enjoy....will enhance the range of experiences you have at college. Interpersonal skills will find their way into both your academics and play. To the extent you can develop good social skills, you will broaden your opportunities and nurture a sense of belonging and connection, resolve conflicts, and perhaps take initiative as a leader. Satisfying social skills are very important for your overall well-being.

The elements of social an emotional intelligence combine and work with one another wherever you are, wherever you go. They are part of how you feel about yourself, manage your life, get along with your family, select your friends, study and learn, behave at a party, complete your tasks at work, and participate in a sport. Indeed, so much of your life's success is dependent upon your social and emotional intelligence.

Many students are truly surprised to learn how important SEI is for their college success, both academically and socially. Now you know.

As you venture into the world of higher education, call on the power of your social and emotional skills to transform your experience. Access and trust your personal strengths to support and guide you all through college. They will enrich your world, stay with you forever, and continue to grow throughout your life, especially if you nurture them.

Have a wonderful journey.

Consider This: In what areas do you consider yourself strong, socially and emotionally? How so? What competencies would you like to strengthen as you move forward in college and in your adult life?

NOTES

Chapter 1   Warm Up: Pumping Your Personal Powers

1. Goleman, Daniel, *Emotional Intelligence: Why It Can Matter More Than IQ*, Bantam Books, 1995.
2. Mayer D., Caruso, R. & Salovey, P. "Emotional intelligence meets traditional standards for intelligence." *Intelligence,* Vol 27, 1999, pp. 267-298.
3. Goleman, Daniel, 1995.
4. In 2015, I collected and reviewed responses from approximately 200 faculty colleagues across academic disciplines at Nassau Community College in Garden City, NY for input and opinions on the causes of student failure or poor academic performance in their classes.

Chapter 2   So Many Ways to Be Smart: Multiple Intelligences and You

1. Cherry, Kedra, "Alfred Binet and the History of I.Q. Testing," www.verywellmind.com, updated 6/13/19.
2. Wechsler, D. (2014). Wechsler Intelligence Scale for Children-fifth edition. Bloomington, MN: Pearson.
3. Gardner, Howard, *Frames of Mind: The Theory of Multiple Intelligences*, Basic Books, 1983.
4. Gardner, Howard, *Intelligence Reframed: Multiple Intelligences for the 21st Century*, Basic Books, 1999.
5. Gardner, Howard, *New Horizons in Theory and Practice*, Basic Books, 2006.
6. Hedlund, Jennifer & Sternberg, Robert, "Too Many Intelligences?" *The Handbook of Emotional Intelligence*, edited by Reuven Bar-On and James Parker, Jossey-Bass Books, 2000, pp.136-167.
7. Goleman, Daniel, *Working with Emotional Intelligence*, Bantum Books, 1998.
8. Elias, Maurice & Zins, J.E. & Weisberg, R. et al, *Promoting Social and Emotional Learning: Guidelines for Educators*, Association for Supervision and Curriculum Development, 1997.

Chapter 3   SEI: What Is It and Why Does It Matter So Much?

1. 1 I compiled responses on the importance of developing social and emotional skills in college classrooms from a variety of professional conferences at which I presented.
2. Goleman, Daniel, *Emotional Intelligence: Why It Can Matter More Than IQ*, Bantam Books, 1995.
3. Salovey, P. & Mayer, J.D, "Emotional Intelligence." *Imagination, Cognition and Personality*, vol 9, no. 3, pp. *185-211*.
4. Parker, James & Duffy, John & Wood, Laura, et al, "Academic achievement and emotional intelligence: Predicting the successful transition from high school to university." *Journal of the First Year Experience*, vol 17, no 1, pp. 67-78.
5. The SEI factors identified here are compiled and integrated from the works of Howard Gardner, Daniel Goleman, Mayer, Caruso, and Salovey, and Reuven Barr-On.

Chapter 4   Look Inside: Being Grounded and Self-Aware

1. Kadison, Richard and DiGeronimo, Theresa, *College of the Overwhelmed: The Campus Mental Health Crisis and What to Do About It*, Josey Bass, 2004, p.156.

2. Goleman, Daniel, *Emotional Intelligence: Why It Can Matter More Than IQ,* Bantam Books, 1995, p.48.
3. Liberman, M.D,. et al, "Social cognitive neuroscience; A review of core processes." *Annual Review of Psychology,* v58, n25, 2007, pp. 9-89.
4. Guest, Judith, *Ordinary People,* Viking Penguin, Inc., 1976.
5. The writing of linguistics expert and author Deborah Tannen, Ph.D, has helped us understand the different styles, motivations, and objectives in the conversation of men and women.
6. Goldsmith, Barton, Ph.D., "Talk About Your Problems, Please." www.psychologytoday.com, March 3, 2011.
7. Thurman, Howard, Baccalaureate Address, Spellman College, May 4, 1980. Jo Moore Stewart, Editor, Spellman Messenger.

Chapter 5   Keep a Lid On: Regulating Emotions in School

1. Linehan, M. & Goodstein, J.L, et al, "Reasons for staying alive when you are thinking of killing yourself: The reasons for living inventory." *Journal of Counseling and Clinical Psychology,* vol 51, 1983, pp. 276-286.

2. Lazarus, R.S. & Folkman, S. *Stress Appraisal and Coping*, Springer, 1984. pp.150-178.
3. Lee, Megan & Bradbury, Joanne, "Five Types of Food to Increase Your Psychological Well-Being," www.MedicalXpress.com, Sept. 10, 2018.
4. www.choosemyplate.gov.
5. Seligman, Martin, Ph.D., *Learned Optimism: How to Change Your Mood and Your Life*, Random House, 2006. p 101

Chapter 6 Reach for the Stars: Setting Your Goals

1. Rogers and Hammerstein, "South Pacific." Original Cast Recording, 1949. www.allmusicals.com/lyrics/rogersandhammerstein.sourthpacific/happytalk.htm
2. Matthews, Gail, Goal Research Summary: Paper presented at the 9th Annual International Conference of Psychology Research Unit of Athens Institute for Education and Research (ATINER) Athens, Greece, 2015.
3. Liff, Suzanne B., "Social and Emotional Intelligence: Applications for Developmental Education." *Journal of Developmental Education*, vol 25, issue 3, 2003, pp 28-34.
4. Duckworth, Angela & Peterson, Christopher et. al, "Grit: Perseverance and Passion for Long

Term Goals." *Journal of Personality and Social Psychology*, vol 92, n 6, 2007, pp1087-1101.

5. Synder, C.R., *The Psychology of Hope: You Can Get There From Here.* New York Free Press, 1994.

6. Seligman, Martin, Ph.D., *Learned Optimism: How to Change Your Mood and Your Life*, Random House, 2006.

Chapter 7   Stay on Top of It:
Strategies for Self-Monitoring

1. Young, D., & Ley, K., "Developmental students don't know that they don't know. Part 1: Self regulation." *Journal of College Reading and Learning*, vol 31, 2000, pp. 54-57.

2. Liff, S., & Stern, J., *Contexts: Reading in the Disciplines*, McGraw-Hill, 2016, p. 8.

Chapter 8   Hold Yourself Accountable:
Self-Monitoring on a Deeper Level

1. Goleman, Daniel, *Emotional Intelligence: Why It Can Matter More Than IQ*, Bantam Books, 1995.

2. In 2016 I developed and disseminated an online questionnaire to the faculty at Nassau Community College. It is a suburban, commuter college, attended by about 23,000 full and

part time students. The questionnaire focused on professors' perceptions for the causes of student success and failure in their classes.
3. Gray, Barbara, "Avid cellphone use by college kids tied to anxiety, lower grades." Health Day News, 12/12/13.
4. Lepp, Andrew & Barkley, Jacob, et al, "The relationship between cell phone use and academic performance in a sample of US college students." *Sage Open*, 5.1, 2015.
5. Manktelow, James and Carlson, Amy. "Overcoming Procrastination," www.MindTools.com, 2019.
6. Lay, Clarry H. "At last, my research article on procrastination,"*Journal of Research in Personality*, vol 20, n 4, December 1986, pp. 474-495.
7. Chick, Nancy. "Metacognition: Thinking About One's Thinking." http://cft:vanderbilt edu/ guides- sub-pages/metacognition/ 4/8/2015

Chapter 9   Feel for Others: Being Empathic

1. Some thoughts here were inspired from an article found on http://www.skillsyouneed.com/ips/ empathy.html#ixzz3Xs4gsZDp and from…
2. Goleman, Daniel, *Working with Emotional Intelligence*, Bantam, 1998, pp.133-146.

3. Goleman, Daniel, *Emotional Intelligence,* Bantam, 1995.

4. Hastings, Paul and Zahn-Wexler, Carolyn, et al, "The development of concern for others in children with behavioral problems," Developmental Psychology, vol 36, n 5, 2000. pp. 531-546.

5. Salem, Richard, "Empathic Listening." Beyond Intractability, www.beyond intractability.org/ print/2620, July 2003.

Chapter 10   You're Not Alone: Forging Social Skills and Making Connections in College

1. Carnegie, Dale, How to Win Friends and Influence People, Simon and Schuster, 1936. Wikipedia notes that with 15 million copies sold worldwide, this is one of the bestselling books of all time. In 2011 it was #19 on Time Magazine's list of the 100 most influential books.

2. Bayer, Lew and Peterson, Cindy Ann, et al, *The Power of Civility: Top Experts Reveal the Secrets to Social Capital,* Thrive Publishing, 2011.

3. Ricci, Ron and Wiese, Carl, *The Collaboration Imperative: Executive Strategies for Unlocking Your Organization's True Potential,* "Four Traits of Collaborative Leaders." Cisco Systems, 2011.

4. Inspired by a point expressed in an online help guide article called "Conflict Resolution Skills" by Jeanne Segal and Melinda Smith on www.helpgude.org/articles/relationships/conflict-resolution-skills htm. Last updated 2/2015.

5. Segal and Smith, "Conflict Resolution Skills," See above.

6. Fulghum, Robert, *All I Really Need To Know I Learned in Kindergarten*, Villard Books, 1998.

Index